INFORMATION TECHNOLOGY
AND
LIBRARY AUTOMATION

INFORMATION TECHNOLOGY AND LIBRARY AUTOMATION

T. Bala Theresa
C. Ratna Kumari
Dr. B.A. Rani

Commonwealth

Information Technology and Library Automation

First Published : 2011

ISBN 978-81-311-0380-7

Published by :
COMMONWEALTH PUBLISHERS PVT. LTD.
4831/24, Prahlad Street,
Ansari Road, Darya Ganj,
New Delhi - 110002
Ph. : 23272541, 23257835
Fax : 91- 011- 23257835
e-mail : commonwealthbooks@gmail.com

Laser Typesetting by :
Dimple Computers
Delhi

Printed at :
Roshan Offset Printers
Delhi

Dedicated

To

Prof. Sasikala C.

Dept. of Library and Information Science
Andhra University
Visakhapatnam, A.P.

Prof. Kamaiah P.

(Retd.) Professor

Dept. of Library and Information Science
Sri Krishnadevaraya University
Ananthapur, A.P.

Who does not thank for little will not thank for much.

~Estonian

Preface

"Books are the quietest and most constant of friends; they are the most accessible and wisest of counselors, and the most patient of teachers."

— *Charles W. Eliot*

Library Science and Information Science are two closely related and often intersecting disciplines that deal primarily with the organization and retrieval of information. Library Science is an interdisciplinary science incorporating the humanities, law and applied science and studying topics related to libraries; the collection, organization and dissemination of information resources; and the political economy of information. Library science has also historically included archival science, although a conceptual distinction between libraries and archives has evolved over time.

Library science is constantly evolving, incorporating new topics like Information Technology-Database Management. Information science is an interdisciplinary science primarily concerned with the collection, classification, manipulation, storage, retrieval and dissemination of information. Information science studies the application and usage of knowledge in organizations, and the interaction between people, organizations and information systems. It is often, though not exclusively, studied as a branch of computer science or informatics and is closely related to the cognitive and social sciences.

Information Technology is not just about computers. More than any other recent development, the computer and specifically Internet-related technology, have changed the way humans interact with the world, information, and each other. To understand social change in the digital age and the implications for information professionals, it is necessary to have a broad understanding of technology. This book will cover the history and development of computers and networking, Internet technologies, and describe some of the electronic tools that are found in modern libraries. We focus on important concepts. We also deal with the implications and consequences of information technology such as collaboration, Electronic resources etc. The purpose of writing this book is, to upgrade the knowledge about the Information Technology, applied in library and Internet technology, web sites, and present information online in an effective and appealing manner, and to understand enough about the inevitable technological changes in our field, to help the professionals.

Information Retrieval is the science of searching for information in documents, for metadata which describe documents, and searching within databases, whether relational stand-alone databases or hyper textually-networked databases such as the World Wide Web. There is a common confusion, however, between data retrieval, document, information retrieval, and text retrieval, and each of these has its own bodies of literature, theory, praxis and technologies. IR is, like most nascent fields, interdisciplinary, based on computer science, mathematics, science, information, cognitive psychology, linguistics, statistics, physics. Automated IR systems are used to reduce information overload.

Through the advances made in technology, the walls of the classroom and the library have expanded to include the entire world. Technology gives us physical access to a wealth of information. IR has become a challenge in the wake of the explosion of knowledge. However; the information housed on servers throughout the globe, in print/electronic resources is so abundant that finding what they need is a daunting task. Information seekers must possess *information literacy* to discern the authenticity of information before use.

— — —

Information literates access, evaluate and use information from a variety of sources. They are organized investigators who question and wonder, find and sort, consume and gulp information. They think, create, summarize and conclude. They communicate effectively and reflect on the process as well as the product. The natural juxtaposition of information literacy to current educational issues alerts one to the importance of creating information literate learners who will succeed in the Information Age. There are two types of access to information—physical access and intellectual access. Intellectual access however, can be denied to the student who does not possess the cognitive strategies for selecting, retrieving, analyzing, evaluating, synthesizing, creating, and communicating. Web browsers and search engines yield thousands of hits on a variety of subjects. CD-ROM databases hold vast amounts of information. Everything from scholarly works to personal interest is available on the Internet.

Automation and the networking of academic libraries have developed considerably. The reasons for, prerequisites of, and benefits of networking are given. Networking systems at the national and local levels are described, as are the salient features of INFLIBNET. There are also networks, viz., DELNET, CALIBNET, and BONET etc. The libraries are already reaping the benefits of networking. The constraints of networking in Indian academic libraries are explained.

Mention has been made of the basic understanding of the *Open Access Resources*, their availability and accessibility. We are seeing a continual growth of interest across the world in the moves made in recent years to stimulate an 'open access' environment, where all research outputs will be available to everyone free of charge at the point of use.

Researchers now have access to greater volumes of research literature than ever before, but we are still far from a position where every researcher who needs it has ready access to all the literature that may be relevant to their research. The current economic difficulties also bring with them the risk of a cut in the library budgets, and that some of the advances in access over recent years will be reversed.

The *Internet* has had more impact on libraries than any other technology since the creation of the book. It may not alter the fundamental nature of the library, but there is no question that the Internet is changing the roles and expectations of libraries.

The retriever is expected to:

- Learn the importance of measuring and maximizing library service through Internet services.
- Discover new and unique Internet-enabled service roles of libraries—expanding on the Web 2.0 environment etc.
- Gain insight in selecting and creating Internet-enabled service roles.

No library is able to satisfy all the needs of its clientele. This led to the concept of Library Co-operation, which in today's jargon is referred to as Resource Sharing. Library Cooperation remained confined to inter-library loan. Even inter-library loan was not being practiced widely. Internet and other local and national networks have facilitated resource sharing. E-resources which have further facilitated information exchange Emergence of library consortia is a promising development. Advent of ICT has opened up new opportunities for greater cooperation among libraries.

The advancement of *Digital Library* technologies provide an effective medium for Library and Information professionals to reach out to the users as never before. At the same time, the rapid proliferation of the digital resources poses an unprecedented challenge to information professionals in generating efficient information services. The goal of this book is to enlighten librarians, information engineers, educators as well as experts and professionals in other related fields, to get ideas about digital libraries and knowledge organization. This book will generate valuable ideas for advancing services for knowledge creation through research.

We must also bear in mind the fact that while there is going to be a spurt in the e-resources of information, the knowledge centre has to also accommodate the research papers and publications that are piling up in the conventional approach to learning and its dissemination.

The specific objectives of this book are :

- To provide an insight for library professionals.
- To advance in the area of digital libraries and knowledge organization.
- To identify best practices in all the spheres of digital library development and knowledge organization.
- To provide strategic directions for the development of digital libraries.
- To prepare a sustainable knowledge organization framework for the development of digital library.
- To be as a resource tool for the Librarians to provide better services to the information seekers/users, this directly involves for the betterment of the society and our country at large.
- To emphasize the importance of taking an effective strategic approach to the management of the Library.

We hope this humble effort of ours will facilitate the emergence of a new approach to the knowledge management and maximize the services of our fraternity to the information seekers, to enhance their research prospects and help in the Nation's progress.

Bala Theresa T.
Ratna Kumari C.
Dr. Asamptia Rani B.

"Education in its real sense is the pursuit of truth. It is an endless journey through knowledge and enlightment, such a journey opens up new vistas of development of humanism".

—A.P.J. Abdul Kalam

Acknowledgement

"A thankful heart is not only the greatest virtue, but the parent of all other virtues."

— *Cicero*

It is with deepest gratitude that all three of us (Authors) thank almighty God. We appreciate the opportunity to write this book, and hope it will be the beginning of a long partnership among the authors, the publishers, and you, our readers. We thank our respective College Principals, Dr. Philomena, Founder Principal of our St. Ann's College for Women and presently the Director and Principal of Villa Marie College, Hyderabad, Dr. Sr. Anthonamma, the present Principal of our College St. Ann's College for Women, Hyderabad and the Management of JMJ College of Education, Guntur, A.P., for their constant support and encouragement in bringing out this book. We thank our colleagues in our respective Colleges for their moral support and guidance. We place on record our appreciation of Dr. E. Rama Reddy, Librarian, UOH, (Retd.), Prof. N. Laxman Rao, UGC, Emeritus Professor, OU, Hyderabad, Prof. L. S. Ramaiah, (Retd.) Librarian, IFLU and all the Professors in LIS departments of Osmania University, Nagarjuna University, SK University, Madhurai Kamaraj University, friends and fellow Librarians who have helped us directly or indirectly. We are grateful to our parents for what we are today and our family members for their unstinted support and patience for sparing long hours all through this year to bring out this book. Finally we thank the Commonwealth Publishers Pvt. Ltd., New Delhi, for bringing out this book by maintaining good quality and standards, and in a short span of time.

Bala Theresa T.
Ratna Kumari C.
Dr. Asamptia Rani B.

Contents

List of Abbreviations and Acronyms Used

AACR :	Anglo American Cataloguing Rules
AGORA :	Access to Global Online Research in Agriculture
AHDS :	Arts Humanities Data Service
AIDS :	Acquired Immune Deficiency Syndrome
ARPANET :	Advanced Research Projects Agency Network
AERADE :	Aerospace and Defence Resources on the Internet
AICTE :	All India Council for Technical Education
ARC :	Across Archive Search Engine
AJOL :	African Journals on Line
ALA :	American Library Association
A & HCI :	Arts & Humanities Citation Index
BALLOTS :	Bibliographical Automation of Large Library Operations
BASE :	Bielefeld Academic Search Engine
BHEL :	Bharat Heavy Electrical Limited
BONET :	Bombay Library Network
BOAI :	Budapest Open Access Initiative
BLDS :	British Library of Development Studies
CCF :	Common Communication Format

CALIBNET :	Calcutta Library Network
CMC :	Computer Maintenance Corporation
CSIR :	Council of Scientific and Industrial Research
CRS :	Creditor Reporting System
CSNET :	Computer Science Network
CARL :	Colorado Computer Alliance of Research Library
DAC :	Development Assistance Committee
DELNET :	Delhi Library Network
DESIDOC :	Defence Scientific Information and Documentation Centre
DELNET :	Developing Library Network
DOD :	Department of Defence
DOAJ :	Directory of Open Access Journals
DMOZ :	Open Directory Project (ODP), also known as Dmoz
DRDO :	Defence Research Development Organization
ENIVAC :	Electronic Numerical Integrator and Calculation
EJDS :	Electronic Journals Delivery Service
EIFL :	Electronic Information for Libraries
ELDIS :	Electronic Development and Environment Information System.
EII :	Enterprise Information Integration
EDVAC :	Electronic Discrete Variable Automatic Computer
ESAP :	Electronic Supply of Academic Publications
E-Prints :	Electronic Prints
ERIC :	Education Resources Information Centre
ERNET :	Education and Research network

FAO : Food and Agriculture Organization Corporate Statistical Database

FTP : File Transfer Protocol

GDN : Global Development Network

GPSS : Gateway Packet Switching System

GUI : Graphical User Interface

HINARI : Health Internet Work Access to Research Initiative

HTML : Hyper Text Mark Up Language

HIV : Human Immunodeficiency Virus

IAUP : International Association of University of Presidents

IFCU : International Federation of Catholic Universities

IL : Information Literacy

IT : Information Technology

ICT : Information Communication Technology

IMARK : Information Management Resource Kit

IMF : International Monetary Fund

INFLIBNET : Information Library Network

ISC : Indian Science Congress

ISO : International Standards Organization

IASLIC : Indian Association of Special Libraries and Information Centers

ICAR : Indian Council of Agricultural Research

ICSSR : Indian Council of Social Science Research

ICMR : Indian Council of Medical Research

ICMS : Indian Council of Medical Research

ICRISAT : International Crops Research Institute for the Semi-Arid-Tropics

IGNOU :	Indira Gandhi National Open University
INSDOC :	Indian National Scientific Documentation Centre
IP :	Internet Protocol
ISBN :	International Standard Book Number
KWIC :	Key Word in Context
LAN :	Local Area Networks
LABORSTA :	International Labour Organization,
MIT :	Massachusetts Institute of Technology
MARC :	Machine Readable Catalogue
MHRD :	Ministry of Human Resources Development
Melvyl :	is the name of the online catalog of the University of California's library system
NICMAP :	National Information Centre for Machine Tools and Production Engineering
NICNET :	National Informatics Centre
NISO :	National Information Standard Organization
NISSAT :	National Information System for Science and Technology
NCLIS :	National Commission on Libraries and Information Science
NCST :	National Centre for Software Technology
NSFNET :	National Science Foundation Network
OA :	Open Access
OMIS :	Om Information Service
OARE :	Online Access to Research in the Environment
OPAC :	Online Public Access Catalogue
OCLC :	Online Computer Library Center
PER :	Programme for the Enhancement of Research Information

OARE :	Online Access to Research in the Environment
OAIster :	A Union catalog of Millions of Record representing OA Resources
PLOS :	Public Library of Science
PICS :	Platform for Internet Content Selection
RLIN :	Research Library Information Networks
RPCS :	Remote Procedure Calls
RDBMS :	Relational Database Management Systems
ROAR :	Registry of Open Access Repositories
RePEc :	Research Papers in Economics
SCI :	Science Citation Index
SIRNET :	Scientific and Industrial Research Network
SCI :	Social Sciences Citation Index
SDI :	Selective Dissemination Information
SMS :	Short Messaging Services
SPARC :	Scholarly Publishing and Academic Research
SRIM :	Selected Research in Microfiche
STM :	Science Technology and Medicine
SQL :	Structured Query Language
TCP :	Transmission Control Protocol
TEEAL :	The Essential Electronic Agricultural Library
UGC :	University Grant Commission
UNIVAC :	Universal Automation
UNESCO :	United Nations Educational, Scientific and Cultural Organization
UN :	Catalogue of United Nations
USAID :	United States Agency for International Development
UNIBISNET :	United Nations Bibliographic Information Systems

UNIVAC :	Universal Automatic Computer
VSNL :	Videsh Sanchar Nigam Limited
WDI :	World Development Indicators
WWW :	World Wide Web
WAN :	Wider Area Network

1

Information Literacy

"Knowledge without wisdom is a load of books on the back of an ass." *TOI*

Introduction

Recent years have witnessed considerable progress in the area of universalization of primary education in India. The nation has crossed the 50 per cent mark with regards to literacy. Nevertheless, it still has the dubious distinction of having the largest number of illiterates in the world. Although there has been a considerable increase in the infrastructure of the education sector, the goal of providing basic education to all still remains a distant dream. In the changing scenario, there is a growing need to realize the importance of libraries in fulfilling the mission of "Education for All by A.D. 2000." Hence, our policy planners need to deliberate on this issue of utmost importance.

Information Literacy: What does it Mean?

"It is the ability to access, evaluate and use information from a variety of sources". Since information may be presented in a number of formats, the term "information" applies to more than just the printed word. Other literacy's such as visual, media, computer, network, and basic literacy's are implicit in information literacy.

To be information literate, a person must be able to recognize when information is needed and have the ability to locate, evaluate, and use effectively the needed information. Producing such a citizenry will require that schools and colleges appreciate and integrate the concept of information literacy into their learning programs and that they play a leadership role in equipping individuals and institutions to take advantage of the opportunities inherent within the information society. Ultimately, information literate people are those who have learned how to learn. They know how to learn because they know how knowledge is organized, how to find information and how to use information in such a way that others can learn from them. They are people prepared for lifelong learning, because they can always find the information needed for any task or decision at hand.

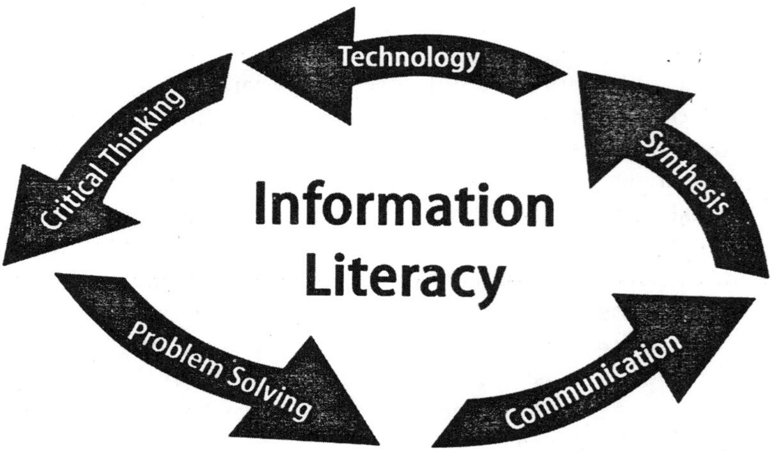

Information Literacy: Origin

The phrase *information literacy* first appeared in print in a 1974 report by Paul G. Zurkowski, written on behalf of the National Commission on Libraries and Information Science. Zurkowski used the phrase to describe the "techniques and skills" known by the information literate "for utilizing the wide range of information tools as well as primary sources in molding information solutions to their problems".

Subsequently a number of efforts were made to better define the concept and its relationship to other skills and forms of literacy. Although other educational goals, including traditional literacy, computer literacy, library skills, and critical thinking skills, were related to information literacy and important foundations for its development, information literacy itself was emerging as a distinct skill set and a necessary key to one's social and economic well-being in an increasingly complex information society.

Another Conception of Information Literacy

This conception, used primarily in the library and information studies field, and rooted in the concepts of library instruction and bibliographic instruction, is the ability "to recognize when information is needed and have the ability to locate, evaluate and use effectively the needed information". In this view, information literacy is the basis for life-long learning.

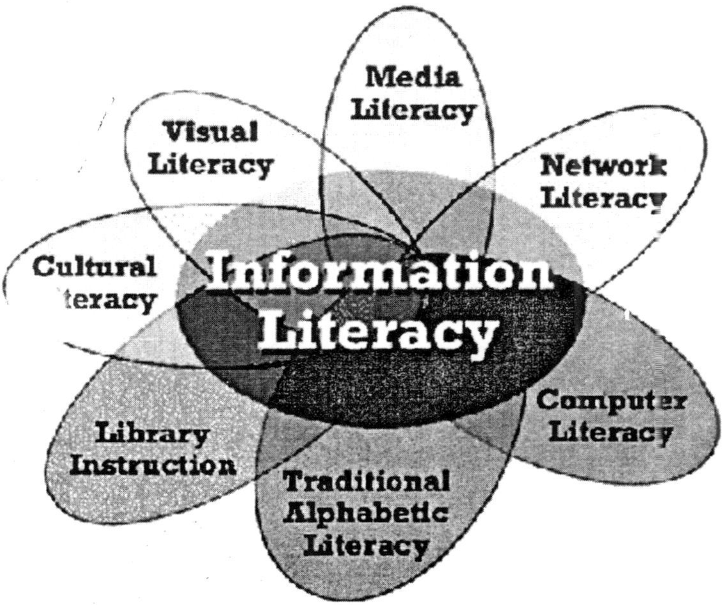

In the publication Information power: Building partnerships for learning (AASL and AECT, 1998), three categories, nine standards, and twenty-nine indicators are used to describe the information literate student. The categories and their standards are as follows :

Category I : Information Literacy

Standards :

1. The student who is information literate accesses information efficiently and effectively.
2. The student who is information literate evaluates information critically and competently.
3. The student who is information literate uses information accurately and creatively.

Category 2 : Independent Learning

Standards :

1. The student who is an independent learner is information literate and pursues information related to personal interests.
2. The student who is an independent learner is information literate and appreciates literature and other creative expressions of information.
3. The student who is an independent learner is information literate and strives for excellence in information seeking and knowledge generation.

Category 3 : Social Responsibility

Standards :

1. The student who contributes positively to the learning community and to society is information literate and recognizes the importance of information to a democratic society.
2. The student who contributes positively to the learning community and to society is information literate and practices ethical behavior in regard to information and information technology.

3. The student who contributes positively to the learning community and to society is information literate and participates effectively in groups to pursue and generate information.

Information Literacy : Components

To this end, IL can be outlined as a "prototype curriculum" that encompasses the concepts of computer literacy, library skills, and "a broader, critical conception of a more humanistic sort", suggesting seven important components of a holistic approach to information literacy:

(1) *Tool literacy* or the ability to understand and use the practical and conceptual tools of current information technology relevant to education and the areas of work and professional life that the individual expects to inhabit.

(2) *Resource literacy* or the ability to understand the form, format, location and access methods of information resources, especially daily expanding networked information resources.

(3) *Social-structural literacy* or understanding how information is socially situated and produced.

(4) *Research literacy* or the ability to understand and use the IT-based tools relevant to the work of today's researcher and scholar.

(5) *Publishing literacy* or the ability to format and publish research and ideas electronically, in textual and multimedia forms ... to introduce them into the electronic public realm and the electronic community of scholars.

(6) *Emerging technology literacy* or the ability to continuously adapt to, understand, evaluate and make use of the continually emerging innovations in information technology so as not to be a prisoner of prior tools and resources, and to make intelligent decisions about the adoption of new ones.

(7) *Critical literacy* or the ability to evaluate critically the intellectual, human and social strengths and weaknesses, potentials and limits, benefits and costs of information technologies.

Over view of the components of Information Literacy/steps of IL

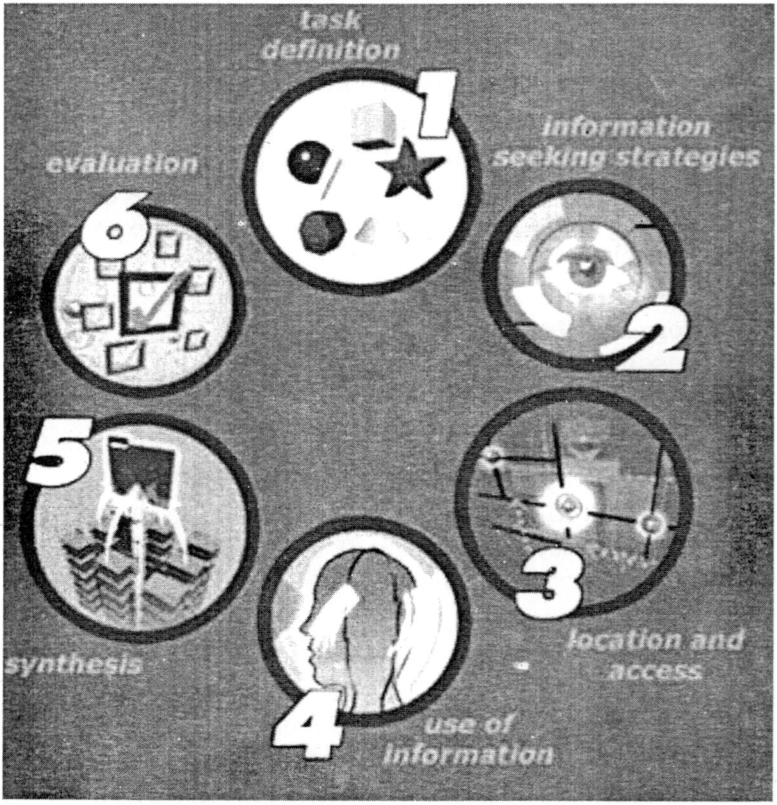

1. The first step in the Information Literacy strategy is to clarify and understand the requirements of the problem or task for which information is sought. Basic questions asked at this stage:

1. What is known about the topic?

   2. What information is needed?
   3. Where can the information are found?
2. **Locating:** The second step is to identify sources of information and to find those resources. Depending upon the task, sources that will be helpful may vary. Sources may include books, encyclopedias, maps, almanacs, etc. Sources may be in electronic, print, social book marking tools, or other formats.
3. **Selecting/analyzing:** Step three involves examining the resources that were found. The information must be determined to be useful or not useful in solving the problem. The useful resources are selected and the inappropriate resources are rejected.
4. **Organizing/synthesizing:** It is in the fourth step this information which has been selected is organized and processed so that knowledge and solutions are developed. Examples of basic steps in this stage are:
   1. Discriminating between fact and opinion.
   2. Basing comparisons on similar characteristics.
   3. Noticing various interpretations of data.
   4. Finding more information if needed.
   5. Organizing ideas and information logically.
5. **Creating/presenting:** In step five the information or solution is presented to the appropriate audience in an appropriate format. A paper is written. A presentation is made. Drawings, illustrations, and graphs are presented.
6. **Evaluating:** The final step in the Information Literacy strategy involves the critical evaluation of the completion of the task or the new understanding of the concept. Was the problem solved? Was new knowledge found? What could have been done differently? What was done well?

Effect on Education

The rapidly evolving information landscape means that education methods and practices must evolve and adapt accordingly. Information literacy must become a key focus of educational institutions at all levels. This requires a commitment to lifelong learning and an ability to seek out and identify innovations that will be needed to keep pace with or outpace changes.

Educational methods and practices, within our increasingly information-centric society, must facilitate and enhance a student's ability to harness the power of information. Key to harnessing the power of information is the ability to evaluate information, to ascertain among other things its relevance, authenticity and modernity. The information

evaluation process is crucial life skill and a basis for lifelong learning.

Evaluation consists of several component processes including metacognition, goals, personal disposition, cognitive development, deliberation, and decision-making. This is both a difficult and complex challenge and underscores the importance of being able to think critically.

INFORMATION LITERACY IN AN INFORMATION SOCIETY

- Recognizes that accurate and complete information is basis for intelligent decision-making.
- Recognizes the need for information.
- Formulates questions based on information needs.
- Identifies potential sources of information.
- Develop successful search strategies.
- Accesses sources of information.
- Evaluate information.
- Organize information for practical application.
- Integrates new information into an existing body of knowledge.
- Uses information in critical thinking and problem solving.

Information Technology : What does it mean?

"It is the study, design, development, implementation, support or management of computer-based information systems, particularly software applications and computer hardware." IT deals with the use of electronic computers and computer software to convert, store, protect, process, transmit and securely retrieve information."

When computer and communications technologies are combined, the result is information technology, or "InfoTech". Information technology is a general term that describes any technology that helps to produce, manipulate, store,

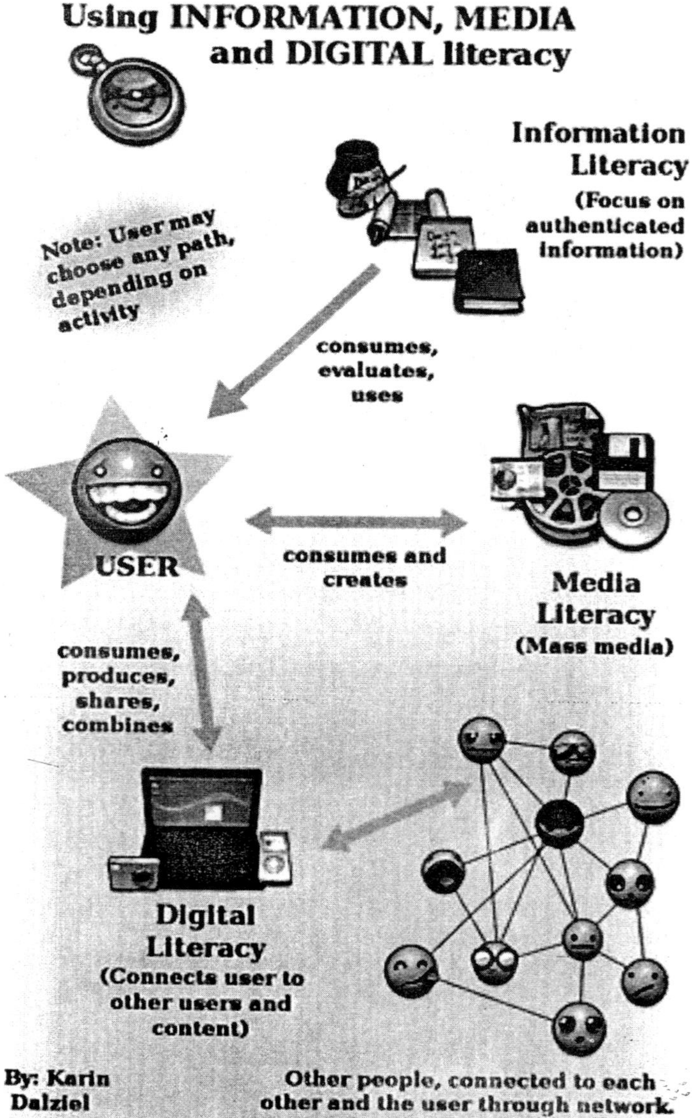
Using INFORMATION, MEDIA and DIGITAL literacy
Information Literacy (Focus on authenticated information)
Note: User may choose any path, depending on activity
consumes, evaluates, uses
USER
consumes and creates
Media Literacy (Mass media)
consumes, produces, shares, combines
Digital Literacy (Connects user to other users and content)
By: Karin Dalziel
Other people, connected to each other and the user through network.

communicate, and/or disseminate information. Presumably, when speaking of Information Technology (IT) as a whole, it is noted that the use of computers and information are associated.

We use the term information technology or IT to refer to an entire industry. In actuality, information technology is the use of computers and software to manage information.

Ways in which Information Technology can Support Learning

- Enables active engagement in construction of knowledge.
- Makes available real-world situations.
- Provides representations in multiple modalities (*e.g.* 3-D, auditory, graphic, text).
- Drills students on basic concepts to reach mastery.
- Facilitates collaborative activity among students.
- Interconnect concepts through hypertext.
- Simulates laboratory work.

Information Literacy and Information Technology

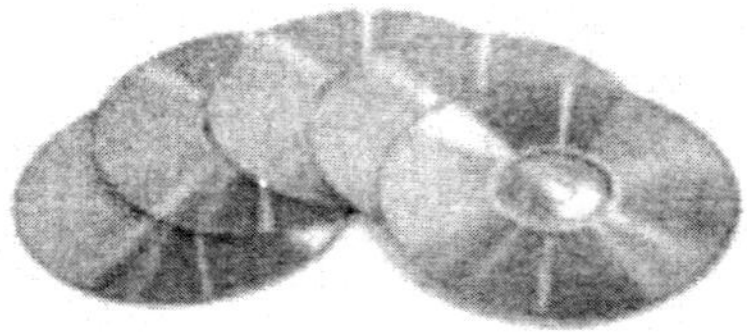

Information technology literacy deals with "an understanding of the technology infrastructure that underpins much of today's life; an understanding of the tools technology provides and their interaction with this infrastructure; and an understanding of the legal, social, economic and public policy issues that shape the development of the infrastructure and the applications and use of the technologies".

Information literacy, on the other hand, deals with content and communication: it encompasses authoring, information finding and organization, the research process, and information analysis, assessment and evaluation. The content in question here can take many forms: text, images, video, computer simulations, and multi-media interactive works. Content can also serve many purposes: news, art, entertainment, education, research and scholarship, advertising, politics, commerce, and documents and records that structure activities of everyday business and personal life.

In an increasingly technological society, the means of authoring, information finding and organization and research, and even information use are increasingly mediated by information technology.

And information technology shapes the channels of publication, access and dissemination of information; the influence, and the intrinsic nature of digital documents, raises new issues in the activities and practices of analysis, assessment, evaluation and criticism.

And much of today's information technology and supporting infrastructure is intended to enable communication, information finding, and information access and information delivery. Teaching of the two sets of literacy skills thus need to be closely coordinated.

Information Technology Literacy

There are two general perspectives on information technology literacy.

The first emphasizes skills in the use of tools:

- Word processing.
- Spreadsheets.
- Basic operation of computers.
- Internet tools such as web browsers and electronic mail.

The key component of information technology literacy is an understanding of the principles of how the technological world works—and I believe it is a mistake to scope this too narrowly to information technology (i.e. computers).

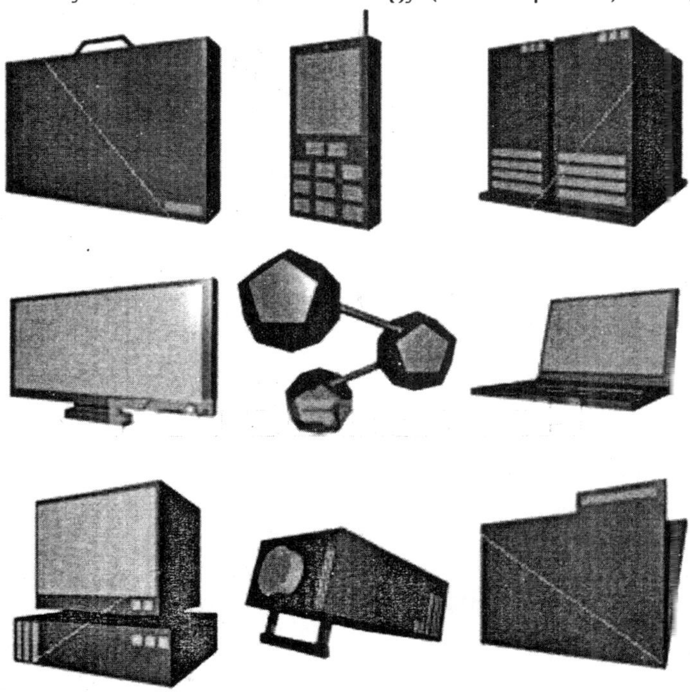

It needs to encompass a rather broad view of the technology infrastructures that support our society, including:

- Computing
- Telecommunications
- Broadcasting
- Publishing
- Electrical power distribution
- Transportation
- Financial Infrastructure

And this understanding needs to encompass not only the technological principles, but also some appreciation of history, economics, social and public policy issues. Information Technology is now pervasively reshaping commerce, communications and society.

The body of knowledge related to text-authoring and critical analytic reading (including the assessment of purpose, bias, accuracy and quality) needs to be extended to the full range of visual (image and video) and multimedia communication genres. This includes an appreciation of interactive media, and also recognition of the fluid nature of any digital forms, plus an understanding of the computer's growing ability to edit or even fabricate what have traditionally been viewed as factual records of events (such as images).

Finally, there are a range of issues related to information policies and practices that are an essential part of information literacy. These include: legal, social, economic, and ethical issues surrounding the ownership and use of intellectual property; privacy questions in the collection and use of information; information authenticity, provenance and integrity; records management, documentation and archiving issues in personal, business, government, and broader cultural contexts; and the management and construction of the social, cultural and intellectual record of discourse.

Information Age provides both opportunities and challenges for future of education and future of society. Information Literacy and Information technology as a theme provides a means to bring about the revolutionary transitions in Economics and Education.

2

Information Technology

"A Wonderful thing about a book, in contrast to a computer screen, is that you can take it to bed with you."

—*Daniel J. Boarstin*

"The Library of the future will be less a place where information is kept than a portable through which students and faculty will access the vast information resources of the world...The Library of the future will be about access and knowledge-management, not about ownership". - Hawkins, 1998.

Introduction

"Information" is the communicating of news, knowledge, or facts. It consists of data endowed with relevance and purpose. Its main function is to present facts so that man's vision is broadened, thereby enabling him to fight against the problems posed by ignorance and superstition. It is therefore considered to be a basic need of man, ranking after air, water, food, clothing, and shelter. Modem means of transport, computers, and telecommunications have reduced the world to a global village, wherein one need only plug in, in order to be connected to the whole world.

It is only recently that information has been recognized as a valuable commodity, and the time may not be far off when information will function as a currency to be exchanged for goods and services all over the world. It is therefore imperative that everybody realize the importance of information and have easy access to it.

The Technology revolution has brought many changes to the way librarians and library staff manage their day provide information to users. Up until ten years ago, libraries were book focused institutions. There were just print card catalogs; online vendor databases had barely become tools in the librarians arsenal to answer questions the internet as we know it now was still years away from practical use. Library acquisitions, cataloging and circulation were done via paper or managed by using ledgers, pens and card pockets. Spread sheets internal databases or other productivity software was never used to manage library data.

We are in the age of networked society where IT in addition to its use in all spheres of human activity has been used extensively to record store and disseminate the information in the digital form. IT has almost converted the world into a global village. The revolution in the IT sector is influencing the information industry also. Libraries are also changing to meet the demand put on them. The new generation whose demand for information is never met is always demanding that traditional libraries should be developed as a well equipped and interconnected as digital libraries. Information Technology is currently taking center stage. The enormous advantage it has in easing the delivery of information around the world as well as the central role of information in the new global economy means that information technology will shape the dynamics of the new millennium.

Information Technology is playing crucial role in contemporary society. It has transformed the whole world into a global village with a global economy which is increasingly dependent on the creative management and distribution of information globalization of world economies has greatly enhanced the values of information to business organizations and has offered new business opportunities. Today, IT provides the communication and analytical power that organizations need for conducting trade and managing business at global level with much ease. To coordinate their world wide network of supplier's distributors and consumers, organizations have developed global information systems that can track orders, deliveries and payment round the clock. This has been possible because of the development of IT in its present form. In broadest sense information technology refers to both the hardware and software that are used to store, retrieve and manipulate information. At the lowest level you have the servers each with an operating system. Installed on these servers are things like database and web serving software. The servers are connected to each other and to users via a network infrastructure. And the users accessing these servers have their pown hardware, operating systems and software tools.

Once basically repositories of vast quantities of information are today becoming producers of information. But Information technology has grown up and so have libraries. We still find hard cover books, videotapes and copying machine among the stacks but now PCS, Lap taps, CD-ROMS/DVDS and Internet access are just as common. For many, the library has become a fully integrated information experience. It is also where many students', users have this first encounters with computers. The Library's technological transformation has not happened overnight "Libraries from 70's to date have had successive generations of automation" according to Peter Young (number of US, National Commission on Libraries and Information Science (NCLIS).

Information Technology (IT) has transformed the functioning and management of modern libraries. Libraries are experiencing enormous changes due to application of new technologies. The rapid rate of technological change has tremendous impact on organization's stake holders, decision makers, library operations, information resources, services, staff competencies and users expectations. Information technology is transforming libraries at a speed unimaginable just a few decades ago. The most pronounced difference between the digital/virtual/hybrid library of today and the traditional library of yester year is the result of rapid pace of technological change taking place in libraries.

The management of massive volume of information and its proliferation into many forms has created the problems of storage, processing, retrieval and dissemination in libraries. The evolution of modern technologies has greatly improved the capabilities of managing this explosive growth of information effectively. Libraries have tried to overcome the problems of information management by adopting modern technologies such as computer technology CD-ROMs, networks etc.

Modern technologies have brought dramatic changes in today's library management and users expectations. Application of IT solutions to library operations and information services is a very complex and challenging process. Libraries are facing a variety of issues, problems, threats and challenges in the introduction, use and management of new technologies. Identifying the problems, understanding the issues and formulation of sound strategies are the keys to the effective management of new technologies in libraries. Libraries intending to use IT applications should have strategic planning, innovative ideas and intelligent strategies for successful implementation and utilization of modern technologies.

In a fast changing, expanding diverse global digital information environment, libraries are facing a variety of new challenges from multiple sectors of the information society.

The major challenges of IT are :

- Information explosion.
- Information and Communication Technology(ICT) revolution.
- Dwindling Library budgets.
- Escalating cost of printed documents.
- Heightened level of users' expectations.
- Changing educational and learning environment.

- Evolution of virtual educational Institutions.
- Changing nature and number of information resources.
- New Patterns of scholarly publishing and communication.
- Development of Digital, Virtual and Hybrid Libraries.
- Online Bookshops.

These challenges have called for reorientation, reengineering and transformation of traditional libraries into modern libraries using new technologies.

Definition of Information Technology

UNESCO defines Information technology as "The Scientific, technological and engineering disciplines and the managerial techniques used in information handling and processing; their applications; computers and their interaction with men and machines and associated social; economic and cultural matters". (Peltu, 1982).

ALA Glossary of Library and Information Science defined IT as "The application of computers and other technologies to the acquisition, organization, storage, retrieval and dissemination of information". (American Library Association, 1983).

According to Olsen (1989), the convergence of three key technologies, viz., computers and telecommunications and microelectronics and the development of a whole range of media (magnetic, optical and now magneto-optical), software, products and services constitutes the package being called information technology.

Kathleen Guinee wrote "By Information technology means the tools we use to perform calculations to store and manipulate text, and to communicate. Some of these twentieth century tools include the adding machine, slide rule and calculator for performing calculations the typewriter and word processing text and the telephone, radio and television for communicating".

Components of Information Technology also known as information and Communication Technology (ICT), IT is defined as the technology required for information processing. In particular the use of computer and computer software to convert, store, and process transmit, and retrieve information. In Information Technology we primarily concentrate on the following technologies :

- *Computer Hardware Technologies:* These technologies include microcomputers, midsize servers and large mainframe systems and the input and output and storage devices that support them.
- *Computer Software Technologies:* Include operating system software, web browsers, software productivity suits and software for business applications.
- *Telecommunication and Network Technologies:* Include telecommunications media, processors and software needed to provide wire-based and wireless access and support for Internet and other networks.
- *Data Resource Management Technologies:* Include database management system, software for the development, access and maintenance of the databases of an organization.

Impact of Information Technology in India

According to N. Vittal, Chairman of the Telecom Commission of India, two major leaps of man were the invention of printing by Gutenberg in the fifteenth century, and the introduction of computers. Technology has advanced quickly since the Second World War. The two main ingredients of technology are computers and communication. When combined, they generate information technology, and this has applications in all walks of life: business, travel, industry, education, shopping, banking, defence, medicine, and leisure.

India is improving its infrastructure of information technology. Its real development is difficult to measure, because the gigantic population acts to the detriment of all plans put forward for the advancement of the nation. In fact,

52 per cent of Indians are literate, and this group is larger than the combined population of the United States and Russia. India's progress should thus be viewed differently. According to the World Bank *Policy Research Bulletin*, only one per cent of India's population has telephones and televisions, as compared with Singapore's 40 per cent, South Korea's 28 per cent, and Taiwan's 33 per cent. Despite this, India has, in absolute terms, more telephones and televisions. The major problem confronting India is its rising population. In order to ensure that the fruits of progress reach each and every person, methods and strategies have to be evolved to curb the population. It needs to be emphasized that the real picture of development should not be hidden in percentage figures. India's manpower with access to education and technology will enable it to emerge as a power in Asia.

Computers made a belated entry into our country, and since then India has not been able to keep pace with developments in other countries. Only 0.1 per cent of the population uses computers, as compared with the US's 24 per cent, Japan's 8 per cent, Germany's 9 per cent, and Singapore's 10 per cent. The planners, policy-makers, and those responsible for the implementation of plans at the central, state, and local levels must decide how to cope with this situation.

Academic libraries and research libraries in India need to coordinate their information requirements and plan for resource sharing. In this regard, the Indian government should allocate funds for INFLIBNET, but the Central Government allocated no such funds in the Union Budget of 1994-95.

Rationale of IT Application in Libraries

Information technology has virtually unlimited potential for a variety of applications in libraries. Several people have given varied reasons for IT applications in libraries.

The main reasons for IT applications in libraries are to :

- Increase the efficiency of library operations.
- Improve the effectiveness of existing services.

- Offer a wide range of new services.
- Perform tasks which cannot be done by the manual system.
- Eliminate duplication of efforts.
- Enable easy participation in resource sharing library networks.
- Enable rapid communication with other libraries
- Generate better management information reports.
- Facilitate marketing of information products and services.
- Provide gateway access to global digital information resources.
- Meet users rising expectations for complex information needs.

In the light of drastically decreasing prices and tremendously increasing capabilities of IT hardware, software and communication equipment, use of new information technologies has become affordable for all types and sizes of libraries. The IT can be used in the following areas:

House-keeping Operations

- Acquisition system.
- Classification.
- Cataloguing.
- Circulation.
- Serial Control.
- Inter Library Loan.
- Management Information.
- Networking and Resource Sharing.
- Information Services.
- In-house Databases.
- Online Public Access Catalogue(OPAC).

- Online Search Service.
- CD-Rom Search Service.
- Internet Service.

Key Factors in IT Implementation

Strategic planning is a key to the successful management of technologies in libraries. Implementation of IT for library operations is a complex and continuous process. It requires imaginative, intelligent planning and huge investment in terms of money as well as human resources. Libraries intending to use IT have to plan systematically well in advance for successful implementation to derive maximum benefits and to minimize the problems.

The following are some of the key factors that should be considered for effective planning and implementation of new information technologies in libraries.

Organizational Environment

The introduction and use of new technologies in libraries will become quite easier and successful only when organizational environment is conducive and supportive. The environment for change is the state of organization's preparedness for acceptance and introduction of change. An environment that supports technological change in an organization's library would be the one in which change is seen as a normal process, and in which the organization's decision makers, library users and library staff are familiar with technological developments and their potential application in the library (Klobas, 1990).

Top Management Support

As IT needs heavy investment, the whole-hearted support of the management is essential for its successful implementation in a library. Top management needs to be fully involved right from the beginning of the technology planning process to the decisions concerning its implementation in library. They should be persuaded, educated and convinced about the potential benefits of IT in various library operations and services to get their support and cooperation. The decision makers in the parent organization need to be made aware of the new developments and opportunities presented by the new technologies, if they are to be support the change proposal and implementation process. They should be well informed about the progress of new technological developments through regular management meetings and sending technology updates news bulletins periodically.

The responsibility of getting management support however has to be taken by professional librarian who must demonstrate a commitment to modernization including the use of it for real benefits to the users' community.

Leadership

The success of IT implementation depends to a great extent on the availability of competent leader with in the library. In order to cope up with the challenges posed by IT, library and information science professionals will have to demonstrate leadership. Librarianship is in a transitory phase characterized by raid changes, in large part enabled by innovation within information and communication technologies. The modern librarianship is to act as a bridge between the society and knowledge seekers, so as to achieve business and educational outcomes in an era that is dominated by information issues.

Creativity refers to the "ability to combine ideas in a unique way or to make unusual associations between ideas." A creative organization develops unique ways of working or novel solutions to problems, but creativity by itself isn't enough. The outcomes of the creative process need to be turned into useful products or work methods, which is defined as innovation. Thus, an innovative organization is characterized by its ability to channel creativity into useful outcomes. When managers talk about changing an organization to make it more creative, they usually mean they want to stimulate and nurture innovation. Innovation is the process of developing a creative idea, so that it can be put to practical use.

IT application in library science can be classified as an organizational change. Organizational Change, "which is any alteration of people, structure, or technology". This change in library and information science needs someone to act as a change agent. It is better that a librarian acts as an "information manager" rather than any IT professional because it is self explanatory that librarians have a better understanding of library functions and services.

So, Librarian must play the role of leader who must be committed and shoulder full responsibility from the planning stage to the successful completion of IT implementation process. He has to plan, direct, control and guides the change management process. He must be able to convince decision makers and communicate to all levels of staff members, interact with users and work in a team environment. The leader must forecast the emerging future technologies and strive to implement and promote their effective use in libraries. He should have people skills, communication skills, knowledge of the library's operations, familiarity with various aspects of library technology; financial resources required human aspects of technological change in libraries. Without librarian's strong commitment, it is difficult to achieve success in introducing, using and maintaining, new technologies in libraries. The success of library automation is increasingly dependent on the commitment of a leader in using new technologies.

Financial Resources

Financial resources are one of the most important factors contributing to the successful implementation of new technologies in libraries. IT needs heavy investment for its implementation in the library. Cost involved in acquisition of hardware, software, databases and computerization, networking and their continued maintenance is very large that many organizations are not able to associate with fast changing to invest in IT. Further, it is difficult to anticipate all costs associated with fast changing nature of emerging dynamic technologies. At the time of allocation of funds, library is being given low priority as compared to other departments in most of the organizations. As a result, libraries are not getting adequate resources required for procuring modern information technologies. Due to fast changing technologies, obsolescence in information technology is so high that it is becoming increasingly difficult for libraries to keep pace with these new technologies without adequate resources.

Adequate funds are essential for implementation of new technologies. Funds must be provided annually install new technology or to maintain existing technology and to update or replace obsolete technology in a regular basis. Financial resources need to be planned carefully taking into account both current and future requirements for managing technological change in libraries. Management must be made aware of the need, usefulness of IT and motivated to allocate more funds for introducing or up gradation of modern technologies in library management.

Today number of organizations namely UGC, CSIR, ICAR, ICMR, ICSSR, NISSAT, AICTE and Department of Science and Technology provide funds for projects submitted for modernization and implementation of new technologies in libraries. Librarians must submit well-prepared project proposals clearly indicating the objectives, activities funds required and time schedules for implementation of new technologies in their libraries.

Staff Competence

One of the most important factors for successful implementation of information technology is the level of competence of the staff (Hoffmann, 1995). Working knowledge of IT in library personnel is fundamental for its successful implementation in library. IT has immense potential for handling various library functions. To make full use of this potential in library management, it is essential, that the library should have adequate personnel who have thorough knowledge of IT application in libraries. But in practice, most of the library personnel do not have adequate level of knowledge and competence of IT applications in libraries.

Working knowledge can be gained only when one is given an intensive training and gets practical hands on experience in using IT.

IT is one of the most rapidly changing areas in the library environment. Keeping up with changes and trends the library technology involves many things, which include :

- Arrange short-term training courses for staff on library automation, databases, LAN, Internet and other timely needed current topics.
- Arrange staff visit to successfully automated libraries.
- Attending professional meetings, conferences and seminars.
- Reading professional literature.
- Personal contacts with experienced fellow professionals.
- Brochures of new software packages, products and services.
- Participation in professional news and discussion groups.
- Subscribing mailing lists.

Staff Involvement

Staff acceptance is another important factor contributing to the successful use of IT in libraries. No new, technologies will be successfully implemented without the acceptance, full support and commitment of all levels of library staff. It is a human tendency to resist change. As some of library still lack knowledge of IT, they are not convinced of the use of IT and so are not willing to respond positively to adapt themselves to the new technologies. There is also a psychological fear in the minds of the library staff that the use of IT in libraries may lead to retrenchment/unemployment. It should be made clear to the staff that IT is used to introduce new services and make improvements and not to reduce with the existing library services/employees. Further they must be convinced that the rapid spread of IT use will lead to a tremendous demand for skilled personnel. Therefore, they must be assuring that no one is going to lose his job as a result of the introduction of IT in libraries.

The success of use of it in library depends on the extent to which supervisory and operational staffs are involved in its planning, design, analysis and implementation. The psychological barriers to change must be cleared in the initial stage involving all the staff in its implementation. Staff involved in IT implementation project need to be trained and must be made aware of the latest developments and be fully involved in the project process and provided guidelines with examples (Msuya, 1990).

Library staff involvement must be multifunctional and multilevel in the technology planning process. Staff involvement in planning a process will create interest, improve motivation and ultimate extend full support and cooperation for successful implementation of new technologies. A number of committees and sub-committees involving key persons from all levels of library staff are to be constituted in planning, decision-making and implementation of new technologies in libraries. Library staff should be kept informed periodically about the plans, decisions activities and progress of the IT implementation process in the library.

Staff Training

Most, often emphasis is placed on the hardware and software aspects of the technology without giving due importance to staff training and development that is needed to ensure effective use of potential benefits of technology. Training library personnel and providing facilities for hands on experience in using computers are important aspects to be given serious consideration. Continuous training on emerging technologies is necessary to develop, maintain and improve skills, knowledge and competencies. An intensive need- based practical oriented training should be imparted to library personnel to instill confidence in order to handle manipulate new technologies. Further, the staff may also be deputed to libraries, which are in advanced state of automation for gaining knowledge and hand-on experience in using IT.

The successful implementation of new technologies can be achieved dully by involving, training and bring the entire library staff together in a team so that they are motivated to contribute greater levels of performance. Library staff should be provided adequate training to have thorough understanding and knowledge of the IT potentials on library and information products and services. The knowledge, skill and interest in various aspects of IT will need to be constantly upgraded among the library staff. Due to fast changing technological developments, continuous in- service training for working library staff is essential for not only to keep them well informed about the latest developments in their fields but also to learn new skills in the use of modern information technologies.

The introduction of new and advanced technologies into the libraries immediately results in different skill requirements. Once the decision to adopt a new technology has been made, management must anticipate and determine, before implementation, the skills necessary to run the new installations efficiently and effectively. Library staff needs to keep abreast of recent developments in technological innovations through a variety of means such as books and journals, professional meetings, and continuing education programs. They must be sent to automated libraries for personal observation and practical experience in handling different technologies. Management must anticipate the skill requirements of new technologies scheduled for implementation and develop operational plans to match existing staff skills through retaining and relocating measures with minimal disruption to operations and minimal adverse effects on the existing staff.

User Education

The success of IT implementation in libraries depends greatly on the extent of users' acceptance and their satisfaction. User is the kingpin of the library. Users should be kept well informed about new technological developments so that they can understand, accept and make more effective use of IT based new services. Informed users can appreciate and may even encourage the library or its parent organization to adopt new technologies. Active marketing approach is the key for user acceptance. Higher levels of user acceptance and utilization can be achieved by well-designed training programme, effective marketing strategy and improved accessibility to computerized services. These services must be accessible and usable not only in the library buildings but also in academic departments and students/hostels/residences round the clock.

Communication

Implementation of new technologies in libraries affects different groups of people in various ways. These groups will need to be informed of different aspects of the process and progress of different stages of IT implementation in library. Effective communication at all stages with all the groups, viz., decision makers, library staff, users and the technology vendors is essential for successful management of technological change in library. There are a variety of communication methods that can be used for different groups for different purposes. They include regular staff meetings, periodical technology update news bulletins and training programmes.

IT Implementation Strategies

Libraries use IT to increase the efficiency and effectiveness of their operations and services. Library developments brought by the new information technologies in the past two decades have clearly demonstrated that the application of IT solutions in library is no longer a matter of choice but is a matter of survival in the solutions in the global digital information era. Managing new technologies has become an expensive, complex and challenging task requiring formulation of sound strategies to achieve success. The management must formulate innovate and intelligent strategies for the successful implementation of IT in libraries.

The following are some of the important strategies to be adopted for successful management of new technologies in libraries.

- Setting objectives.
- Assessment of existing system.
- Identifying priorities.
- Development of specifications for the required system.
- Software selection.
- Requesting Proposals.
- Selection Proposals of Software.

Setting Objectives

For effective implementation of any IT application, the objectives of a new system should be clearly defined. Clearly stated objectives are the keys are successful IT implementation. The objectives must revised/redefined and made as user oriented as possible. List the major and specific objectives for different sections of the library that will be accomplished through the use of technology. The objectives should be specific, realistic and easily measurable in quantitative measures. Well-defined objectives will form sound basis for effective strategic planning of financial resources, activities, processes, procedures and services. The objectives can include offering more efficient and effective delivery of current services or to add new services to help carryout the mission of the library.

Assessment of Existing System

Introduction of new technologies in libraries is a major complex process, which requires through examination and analysis of various aspects and activities. Before introducing any new technology it is useful to do a formal study to investigate the existing system, find out the limitations, examine various options, assess the potential benefits of new technologies and identify the needed resources for implementation of new technologies. This needs to collect the basic statistical information about collections, acquisitions circulations, services and users for complete description of the existing system. The assessment of existing system should involve collecting, organizing and analyzing facts about the current systems' objectives, functions, processing operations, and work flows, size of files, inputs, outputs and resources. It surveys user needs in order to assess their expected services from a new system. User needs assessment can be done either through existing use patterns, interview, observation or surveys. Since ever, the 'user' has been of 'center' of librarianship and information science services and continued as a focus for research. Virtually every development and its implementation in the field of information science have been of the concern towards making it easier for the 'user' to gain access to information. In due course of time, the 'user' as a living person became the focus of attention in information research. Initially, the system and its use and users had been the focus. In recent past, the 'individual user' has been considered as the focus of the whole process and profession of librarianship. The individual user identifies possible sources, differentiates and chooses a few sources locaters or makes contact with them and interacts with the source in order to obtain the desired information the information-seeking behavior dimensions can be categorized as cognitive, affective and situational.

The assessment should be done by a committee consisting of library staff, and computer specialists. Through assessment of the existing system will enable us to study and identify the requirements for the development of logical design of the new system. The strategies or methods to be employed in order to satisfy the Information technology based needs of the information seeking behavior of users is the focus of this study.

Identifying Priorities

Based on the information collected in the previous steps, it is necessary to determine which library function should be automated and in what order of priority. In setting priorities, the factors considered include increased efficiency in manual operations, service improvements, high priority user needs and cost effectiveness.

There are usually three factors that drive automation priorities in the typical library :

- Manual processes that can be performed more efficiently using technology.
- Services or service improvements that are a high priority for users.
- New services or service improvements that provide significant benefit in relation to cost.

The functions most often automated include development of databases, Online Public Access Catalogue (OPAC), acquisitions, circulation and serials control (Cohin et al, 1998).

Development of Specifications for the Required System

Once the decision has been made regarding what functions are to be automated, the next step is the development of specifications and features required of a system. The detailed system specifications are essential to get the best system suitable for the library. The detailed specifications should outline all of the functional requirements and features required in a system. A committee may be formed to coordinate the development of specifications for a required system. Functional sub-committees involving the staff of all user departments may be formed for defining the functional requirements and developing specifications for their respective functions. These specifications will be reviewed and finalized after necessary modifications and revisions. The requirements are to be ranked as mandatory and desirable based on their relative importance. Many problems encountered later can be avoided if the system requirements are clearly identified and specified.

The specifications will serve as important guidelines in negotiating with the system supplier as well as a basis for final selection of the software package.

3

Library Automation

"The more we reduce ourselves to machines in the lower things, the more force we shall set free to use in the higher."

—Anna C. Brackett

Brief History of Library Automation 1930 - 1996

The Beginnings of Library Automation: 1930-1960. It could be said that library automation development began in the 1930's when punch card equipment was implemented for use in library circulation and acquisitions. During the 30's and early 40's progress on computer systems was slow which is not surprising, given the Depression and World War II. In 1945, Vannevar Bush envisioned an automated system that would store information, including books, personal records and articles. Bush (1945) wrote about a hypothetical "memex" system which he described as a mechanical library that would allow a user to view stored information from several different access points and look at several items simultaneously. His ideas are well known as the basis for hypertext and computers for their operations. The first appeared at MIT, in 1957, with the development of COMIT, managing linguistic computations, natural language and the ability to search for a particular string of information. Librarians then moved beyond a vision or idea for the use of computers, given the technology, they were able make great advances in the use of computers for library systems.

In a broad sense, between 1954 and today, library automation has evolved through three incremental phases—efficiency of internal operations, access to local resources and access to resources outside the library. Thus, a clear shift can be seen from local concerns to global concerns. According to Borgman we are now at a stage where interoperability among systems and services has become the key objective. However, while this may be true for the developed world, many libraries in the developing world are still largely seeking automation solutions to improve the efficiency of local operations, rather than improved access to resources outside their libraries.

Early efforts to automate library and services using computers began during mid-1950s, almost a decade after digital computers became available. It is convenient to view the history of library automation in three distinct phases: the first, during the period 1954 - 70; the second, during 1970 - 90; and the current phase, from 1990 onwards. Each of these phases has been influenced by the technologies (hardware and software) available at those times; the social and political influences on education and research; and the convergence of media, computer, and communication technologies that took place over these years.

Lead to an explosion of library automation in the 60's and 70's. Library Automation Officially is Underway: 1960 - 1980 The advancement of technology lead to increases in the use of computers in libraries. In 1961, a significant invention by both Robert Noyce of Intel and Jack Kirby of Texas Instruments, working independently, was the integrated circuit. All the components of an electronic circuit were placed onto a single "chip" of silicon. This invention of the integrated circuit and newly developed disk and tape storage devices gave computers the speed, storage and ability needed for on-line interactive processing and telecommunications. The new potential for computer use guided one librarian to develop a new indexing technique. H.P. Luhn, in 1961, used a computer to produce the "keyword in context" or KWIC index for articles appearing in Chemical Abstracts. Although keyword indexing was not new, it was found to be very suitable for the computer as it was inexpensive and it presented multiple access points. Through the use of Luhn's keyword indexing, it was found that librarians had the ability to put controlled language index terms on the computer. By the mid-60's, computers were being used for the production of machine readable catalog records by the Library of Congress. Between 1965 and 1968, LOC began the MARC I project, followed quickly by MARC II. MARC was designed as way of "tagging" bibliographic records using 3-digit numbers to identify fields. For example, a tag might indicate "ISBN," while another tag indicates "publication date," and yet another indicates "Library of Congress subject headings" and so on. In 1974, the MARC II format became the basis of a standard incorporated by NISO (National Information Standards Organization). This was a significant development because the standards created meant that a bibliographic record could be read and transferred by the computer between different library systems. ARPANET, a network established by the Defense Advanced Research Projects Agency in 1969 brought into existence the use of e-mail, telnet and ftp. By 1980, a sub-net of ARPANET made MELVYL, the University of California's on-line public access catalog, available on a national level. ARPANET would become the prototype for other networks such as CSNET, BITNET and EDUCOM. These networks have almost disappeared with the evolution of ARPANET to NSFNET which has become the present day Internet. During the 1970's the inventions of the integrated computer chip and storage devices caused the use of minicomputers and microcomputers to grow substantially. The use of commercial systems for searching reference databases (such as DIALOG) began. BALLOTS (Bibliographical Automation of Large Library Operations) in the late 1970's was one of the first and later became the foundation for RLIN (the Research Libraries Information Network). BALLOTS was designed to integrate closely with the technical processing functions of the library and contained four main files: (1) MARC records from LOC; (2) an in-process file containing information on items in the processing stage; (3) a catalog data file containing an on-line record for each item; and (4) a reference file. Further, it contained a wide search retrieval capability with the ability to search on truncated words, keywords, and LC subject headings, for example. OCLC, the On-line Computer Library Center began in 1967, chartered in the state of Ohio. This significant project facilitated technical processing in library systems when it started its first cooperative cataloging venture in 1970. It went on-line in 1971. Since that time it has grown considerably, providing research and utihypermedia. In order to have automation, there must first be a computer. The development of the computer progressed substantially from 1946 to 1961, moving quickly though a succession of vacuum tubes, transistors and finally to silicon chips. From 1946 to 1947 two significant computers were built. The ENIAC I (Electronic Numerical Integrator and Calculator) computer was developed by John Mauchly and J. Presper Eckert at the University of Pennsylvania. It contained over 18,000 vacuum tubes, weighed thirty tons and was housed in two stories of a building. It was intended for use during World War II but was not completed in time. Instead, it was used to assist the development of the hydrogen bomb. Another computer, EDVAC, was designed to store two programs at once and switch between the sets of instructions. A major breakthrough occurred in 1947 when Bell Laboratories replaced vacuum tubes with the invention of the transistor. The transistors decreased the size of the computer, and at the same time increased the speed and capacity. The UNIVAC I (Universal Automatic Computer) became the first computer using transistors and was used at the U.S. Bureau of the Census from 1951 until 1963. Software development also was in progress during this time. Operating systems and programming languages were developed for the computers being built. Librarians needed text-based computer languages, different from the first numerical languages invented for the number crunching "monster computers", in order to be able to use colitis designed to provide users with the ability to access bibliographic records, scientific and literary information which continues to the present. Library Automation 1980-present the 70's were the era of the dummy terminal that were used to gain access to mainframe on-line databases. The 80's gave birth to a new revolution. The size of computers decreased, at the same time, technology provided faster chips, additional RAM and greater storage capacity. The use of microcomputers during the 1980's expanded tremendously into the homes, schools, libraries and offices of many Americans. The microcomputer of the 80's became a useful tool for librarians who put to them to use for everything from word processing to reference, circulation and serials. On-line Public Access Catalogs began to be used extensively the 1980's. Libraries started to set-up and purchase their own computer systems as well as connect with other established library networks. Many of these were not developed by the librarians themselves, but by vendors who supplied libraries with systems for everything from cataloging to circulation. One such on-line catalog system is the CARL (Colorado Alliance of Research Libraries) system. Various other software's became available to librarians, such as spreadsheets and databases for help in library administration and information dissemination. The introduction of CD-ROMs in the late 80s has changed the way libraries operate. CD-ROMs became available containing databases, software, and information previously only available through print, making the information more accessible. Connections to "outside" databases such as OCLC, DIALOG, and RLIN continued, however, in the early 90's the databases that were previously available on-line became available on CD-ROM, either in parts or in their entirety. Libraries could then gain information through a variety of options. The nineties are giving rise to yet another era in library automation. The use of networks for e-mail, ftp, telnet, Internet, and connections to on-line commercial systems has grown. It is now possible for users to connect to the libraries from their home or office. The World Wide Web which had its official start date as April of 1993 is becoming the fastest growing new provider of information. It is also possible, to connect to international library systems and information through the Internet and with ever improving telecommunications. Expert systems and knowledge systems have become available in the 90s as both software and hardware capabilities have improved. The technology used for the processing of information has grown considerably since the beginnings of the thirty ton computer. With the development of more advanced silicon computer chips, enlarged storage space and faster, increased capacity telecommunication lines, the ability to quickly process, store, send and retrieve information is causing the current information delivery services to flourish. Early efforts to automate library and services using computers began during mid-1950s, almost a decade after digital computers became available. It is convenient to view the history of library automation in three distinct phases: the first, during the period 1954-70; the second, during 1970 - 90; and the current phase, from 1990 onwards. Each of these phases has been influenced by the technologies (hardware and software) available at those times; the social and political influences on education and research; and the convergence of media, computer, and communication technologies that took place over these years.

The nineties are giving rise to yet another era in library automation. The use of networks for e-mail, ftp, telnet, Internet, and connections to on-line commercial systems has grown. It is now possible for users to connect to the libraries from their home or office. The World Wide Web which had its official start date as April of 1993 is becoming the fastest growing new provider of information. It is also possible, to connect to international library systems and information through the Internet and with ever improving telecommunications. Expert systems and knowledge systems have become available in the 90's as both software and hardware capabilities have improved. The technology used for the processing of information has grown considerably since the beginnings of the thirty. Library automation which started in late 70s in few special libraries has now reached most of the university libraries. It is yet to take off in college libraries in India owing to various problems. To identify the barriers, analyze the convenient steps in automating the library and the technology available.

Why library Automation

Even though this question seems to be very fundamental it is essential to emphasize this aspect as the library automation is yet to take off in majority of the Indian libraries. Secondly, while justifying need for library automation more than cost-effectiveness the benefits derived by the library users become the major consideration. Since library does not happen to be an economic entity such benefits need to be looked at in a different perspective. To appreciate the advantages it becomes necessary to highlight the different levels of library automation. For convenience it can be visualized at four levels:

- Library cataloging system.
- House keeping operations and networking.
- Development of CD-ROM library/products.
- E-mail system and internet.

The library catalogue or index to the collection forms the base for most of the library activities such as acquisition, reference, bibliographic service, inter-library loan etc. The users of library card catalogue will appreciate how fast the retrieval is, search and printing in automated environment. If the same system is available in network environment, users can have simultaneous access to the same database. From the library staff point of view the cumbersome job of printing the cards and their subsequent filing gets eliminated. Also, it conserves space and saves stationary.

The second level automation will be to use software which can handle all the house keeping operations of the library such as acquisition, circulation and serial control thus creating a network within the library or becoming part of the existing network of the institution. Networking of computers within an organization helps the users to browse the cataloguing system from any of the **workstation/terminal**.

A very handy technology available for library is the CD-ROM products which can be considered at the third level. The development of CD-ROM collection not only conserves space but also provides multi-user access in network environment.

There are many self-tutorial CD-ROMS available with multi-media effect. Libraries facing high incidence of mutilation of materials will benefit from such electronic products. Also people doing empirical research can download data and directly take it to other software platform for analysis and making graphical presentation.

Other technology which libraries can make use of is the e-mail system. This not only reduces the recurring expenditure but also be effective and fast. Sending reminders for non-receipt of journals by e-mail has proved to be very cost-effective. In addition to this, sharing of resources among libraries become easy. Few public domain e-mail software are available and there will be no additional expenditure incurred.

Another technology which has revolutionized the information world is the development of internet. Subscribers of internet, in addition to getting access to various public domain databases and services, will also get free e-mail and fax facility. Some publishers have started giving content pages of journals and libraries having subscription to such journals can also have full text of the articles. Many academic and research institutes have given free access to their working papers.

Attempts towards Automation in Indian Libraries

The scientific and technical libraries working under such R&D institutions as CSIR, ICMR, ICAR and DRDO have taken the lead in library automation. Notable among public sector libraries are BHEL, R&D and SAIL.They have funded several training programs and software development projects which have played an important role in increasing awareness of the potential of the new technologies. Their main emphasis was on database development and information retrieval services. Unfortunately, the academic libraries have made little progress in this direction. The reasons for the slow pace of automation in academic libraries are the following :

- Academic libraries in India function in a relatively less autonomous environment.

- The academic libraries are a comparatively smaller unit within a larger setup.
- Libraries have to compete for scarce resources.
- Undergraduates outnumber postgraduates, faculty, and research staff.
- Academic libraries are not under as much pressure to improve their services as are scientific and technical libraries.

Barriers of Library Automation

Following could be the few possible barriers of library automation :

(i) Fear of adverse impact on employment.

(ii) Apprehension that the technology could be too expensive.

(iii) The library staff has to undergo extensive training

(iv) Lack of support from the management, may be owing to budget constraints.

(v) Fifth reason could be retrospective conversion of data.

Let us examine each of the points. If we analyze the various jobs such as book acquisition, technical processing, circulation and reference service one can conclude that human interference is necessary at each and every step. The only area where substantial manpower can be saved is the cataloguing. The data entered at the time of ordering can be used for cataloguing with some updation would eliminate multiple card preparation and subsequent filing. The manpower thus saved can be utilized in retrospective conversion and later on for analytical cataloguing or introducing new services. Therefore, there will be no adverse impact on employment.

There is an apprehension that the technology, both hardware and software would be expensive and unaffordable. The cost of hardware and software depends on the level of automation. From the user point of view cataloguing system is most important and also forms the base for other library activities. Keeping these two points in view UNESCO developed PC based software titled 'CDS/ISIS' and is available at a very nominal price to all the libraries in developing countries. For details librarians may contact ATIRA/NISSAT.

This software which works on a simple IBM compatible PC/XT is also available on UNIX and NOVELL platform. Recently the WINDOWS version has also been released. This software can export data in ISO 2709 format and therefore at later stage if one decides to go in for some other software, data transfer poses no problem. INFLIBNET has developed public domain library software titled 'ILMS' which is available on DOS AND UNIX platform. With the recent government policy the PCs and other accessories have become affordable.

The in-house training for handling the software is usually provided by the developers and one can choose the software which can suit their budget. However, training for CDS/ISIS is available at INSDOC, INFLIBNET and DRTC. For further information on training programmes one can contact NISSAT. The training of library staff also depends on the level of automation. If one decides to go only for cataloguing a minimum training of one or two week's duration will enable the librarians to develop a database and maintain it. With this basic training one can easily transfer the same data on a server/main machine in a network environment. The job becomes easy as most of the institutions have systems department with computer professionals maintaining the network.

Fourthly lack of support from the management, may be owing to budget constraints, will be one of the barriers. Here the role of librarians becomes crucial in convincing the management that the users of libraries will also be the major beneficiaries of automation. Also, the skill and initiative play a major role in convincing the management.

The fifth reason could be retrospective conversion of data. As mentioned earlier the manpower saved could be utilized for retrospective conversion and later on for analytical cataloguing. However, most of the libraries have taken time bound project for this purpose.

Selection of Library Software

As mentioned earlier, if a library wants to make a beginning; CDS/ISIS is best suited as it involves minimum investment on both hardware and software. Once a database with bibliographic details is developed, the same data can be used for circulation activities. Here the selection of software becomes crucial because CDS/ISIS can efficiently handle only the cataloguing system. Following criteria might help the librarians to select the right software for other housekeeping operations :

1. Who are the developers, whether an institution, or reputed company or few individuals. The preference is for institution and second preference is for the reputed company. One has to be skeptical about the software developed by individuals as there will be no continuity.
2. How many times the software has been revised since the time of its first launch.
3. How many parameters are available for each module? More the parameters better will be the flexibility and needs no or minimum customization.
4. Whether the software has facility to import bibliographic data available in ISO-2709 format and similarly export of data in this format.
5. Training and guidance after installation.
6. Whether available on major operating systems.
7. Whether it is web interface.
8. Whether it can be interfaced with the e-mail system of the campus network.
9. Whether it has taken care of Y2K compliant.
10. How many installations it has got in the country, since when and major clients.

11. Whether it can offer OPAC and different rights to different logins.

Networking is a key for the development of library automation. New developments have been made in theories and practices in library automation, networking and database development. In the future; we should make our efforts to establish the "Library Information Network", realizing collaborative library operation in a network environment. Libraries should switch their focus from collection to access, from isolated management to cooperative management, from traditional document services to networked information services, from closed door policy to open door policy.

It attempts to give some idea for beginners in library automation. Even though wide range of technology/products are available, it is necessary for librarians to keep a watch on the developments and to choose appropriate technology depending on the needs. Also, it is very important for librarians to interact with computer professionals as the library automation at all levels needs good co-ordination among both these professionals.

Data Exchange

We have already seen how the gradual convergence of computing and communications technologies improved access to information resources within and outside of libraries. In the early days, data exchange between systems was limited to batch tape loading and custom programming. Loading records from shared cataloguing systems into the early automated library systems was difficult, because of proprietary forms and inconsistent application of standards. Even with standards in place, differences interpretation and application rules, and differences in system implementation, made the exchange and merging of records a nontrivial task. An important international standard for the exchange of bibliographic records between systems- the ISO-2709 format – was defined during 1970 - 90.

One of the first breakthroughs is automated bibliographic data exchange was the Linked systems project, begun in themed- 70s by the Library of Congress and the major U.S. Bibliographic utilities.

Integrating other Online Resources

While the online catalogue was a huge advance, it did not completely meet the needs of some categories of library users. It was only in the late 1980s and early 1990s that these abstracting and indexing databases were mounted for interactive public access, opening up journal literature in the same way that the online catalogue opened up monographic literature.

Technology and Environment

Computer technology for the part of this period (1970 - 90) was dominated by minicomputers, with the PDP-11, VAX-11, Wang and HP-3000 series machines being the most popular, ones. The years 1970 - 90 also saw the emergence of new software languages.

Networking Technologies

The period 1970 - 90 also saw many important developments in networking technology- developments that, in fact, provided the building blocks for the Internet and the World Wide Web. Communication of data over the Internet is based on this technology even to this day.

Packet-switching allows data to be broken up into packets, with each packet containing information about the sources of the packet, its destination and its sequence in the total set of packets comprising the file or message.

Tymnet and Telent were two important packet-switched data networks of the 1970s and 1980s. During the 1970s and 1980s organizations that needed to network their corporate offices with their branch offices in other cities.

Local Area Networks (LAN) or networks that interconnect personal computers, file servers printers, disk drives and CD towers in a single building or in a groups of closely located buildings, also became possible due to the development of appropriate communications hardware and software, standard networking protocols and media during the 1970s and 1980s.

The Birth of the Internet and the World Wide Web

The 1960s and 1970s saw important initiatives by the US Department of Defense and the Agency for Advanced Research Projects that ultimately led to the Evolution of the Internet. The DOD wanted to create a network that would continue to operate even if part of the network was damaged during hostilities in the event of war. Internet history came in the early 1980s with the development of the Transmission Control Protocol/Internet Protocol (TCP/IP) by Vincent Cerf and his graduate students at the University of California at Los Angels. The TCP/IP suite of protocols became the crucial technology that allowed different computers to "talk" with each other, i.e., exchange data among themselves.

Development since 1990

The opening up of the Internet to the world at large in the late 1980s and its rapid percolation in the 1990s, together with the development of protocols, software, hardware and standards that make up the World Wide Web.

The types of library automation systems will be reviewed, emphasizing the concept of an integrated library automation system and its advantages compared to the standalone systems. The sub-systems of a typical library automation system will then be considered. Libraries exist in different organizational settings.

Library should automate its operations and services are a question that is rarely asked. Information resources are increasingly being seen as valuable national resources and ones that must be shared among the different seekers such resources. The choices in balancing services to their multiple constituencies influence why and how libraries automate. The effectiveness of a library in balancing its services to multiple constituencies is important for the library to get continued support - political and financial – from the organization it is expected to serve and from its other constituents. The main reasons why libraries seek the application of it solutions are to :

- Obtain increased operational efficiencies.
- Relieve professional staff from clerical chores so that they are available for user oriented services.
- Improve the quality, speed and effectiveness of services.
- Improve access to remote users and other stakeholders rove access to resources on other networks and systems, including the Web.
- Provide new services no hitherto possible.
- Enable rapid communication with other libraries and professional peers.
- Enable their participation in resource-sharing library networks.
- Facilitate wider dissemination of their information products and services.
- Facilitate wider access to information of their clients.
- Improve the management of their physical and financial resources.

The above mentioned reasons are not mutually exclusive. Benefits of the application of IT have been known to have a spillover effect. Also it is well known that a library beginning with one application and raping its benefits, soon begins to look for other areas where IT solutions are possible and useful. In many developing countries users especially in academic and research institutions, have been responsible for initiatives that have led to library automation in these institutions.

Automation of a library involves investments in costly hardware and software and other resources, retraining of staff, and in some cases recruitment of new staff. There could be considerable dislocations in services during the changeover from a non-automated service to an automated service. This is stressful both for library staff and users. The rationale for choosing automated solutions should therefore be clearly understood by the management, library staff at all levels, and users. Ideally, there should be a shared understanding of the rationale and the costs and benefits of automation. Each,

Library is uniquely positioned vis-à-vis its parent organization and its user community and therefore will view its reasons for introspect with the management of the institution it serves and with its clients to determine the benefits that automation may ultimately provide to all concerned and in the prioritization of its automation program. Such introspection and a shared understanding of goals can go a long way in creating a healthy climate in which automation can be planned and implemented.

Library automation systems can be broadly be categorized into two types :

- Standalone systems.
- Integrated systems.

Standalone Systems

These are systems that automate a single library function, e.g., Circulation control.

Integrated System

Integrated library system is one in which all of the functional modules shared a common bibliographic database. An important feature of integrated systems is that there is considerable data exchange taking place between the different sub-systems quite transparently to the user. Genway described the integrated online library system as "a library system that uses a common machine-readable database and has two or more sub-systems operational and accessible online". The integration of a system can be accomplished in different ways. A library can :

- Buy an integrate system, including a number of functional modules, from a single vendor or
- buy different modules from different vendors and interconnect them through local programming efforts. An integrated system is superior in several ways to one that is not integrated.
- Duplication of effort to create and maintain multiple copies of bibliographic records is eliminated in an integrated system.

- Possibility of errors is minimized when records are entered only once, and changes are automatically propagated throughout the system.
- Library staff and patrons can have access to all pertinent information at once location.
- Maintenance and troubleshooting is simpler in an integrated system compared with one that is not integrated.

Integrated systems are particularly useful for library patrons. The privacy of borrowers can be protected by preventing patrons from viewing borrower information. Patrons looking at an integrated system's online catalogue can also see that a book has been ordered but not yet received by the library. In a non-integrated system, such information would be restricted to library staff who would view it only through the acquisitions module.

Integrated systems first made their appearance in mainframe architectures. In such a computing environment, all processing was done within the central host computers. Users interacted with the host through a terminal. User interaction was via PCs or UNIX workstations. Mainframe Software architectures did not support graphical user interfaces In the late 1980s and early 1990s, the original PC networks were based on file-sharing architectures where the server downloaded filed from the shared location to the desktop environment. File-sharing architectures work if shared location to desktop environment. File sharing architectures work if shared usage, update connection, and the volume of data to be transferred are low. In the 1990s, PC LAN computing underwent a change because the capacity of the file sharing became strained as the number of online users grew and GUIs became popular, making mainframe and terminal displays appear out of data. The limitation of file-sharing architectures led to the emergence of a new architecture called the client-server architecture. This approach introduced a database server to replace the file server. Using a Relational Database Management Systems (RDBMS), user queries could be answered directly.

The client server architecture reduced network traffic by providing a query response rather than total file transfer. In client server architectures, Remote Procedure Calls (RPCs) or Standard Query Language (SQL) statements are typically used to communicate between the client and server. The emergence of the Internet and the Web accelerated the move toward client server architectures in the 1990s.

The definition of an integrated system has change from a system that shares bibliographic records among local function and modules to a system that exchanges information with many other systems outside of the library. Some libraries with expanded integrated systems offer patron access through their local online public access catalogues to other bibliographic and non-bibliographic databases both inside and outside the library and to OPACs of other libraries. Most high-end integrated systems today as web-based and client server architecture based.

Library Automation Sub-systems

Library automation systems have viewed as comprising a number of functional sub-systems :

- Acquisitions.
- Cataloguing.
- Circulation control.
- Serials control.
- OPACs.

The acquisition of books and other material triggers all other activities in a library. Once these are acquired they will need to be catalogued, indexed, and prepared for display and browsing on library shelves. The books/material then becomes available for circulation. Serials have unique characteristics and therefore their acquisition and control is managed differently. OPAC is the electronic equivalent of the catalogue card.

Use Scenario in Library Automation

A library seeking to automate was chiefly concerned with its own requirements, conditions and priorities. Little considerations were given to networking with other libraries and resource sharing. Today, however with the increasing need to access external resources, the possibility of shared functionality and the need for exchanges of networking of libraries. We are seeing greater emphasis on automation solutions that enable networking of libraries within an organization and across similar organizations

Automation of Book Acquisition Systems

The acquisition of books, serials and non-book materials (CD-ROMs, microforms, videotapes, etc.) is an important activity of all kinds of libraries, big and small. The acquisitions function includes tasks that require human judgment as well as those that could be classified as clerical. While automation of the acquisitions function can help only marginally in helping to build a sound acquisitions policy, it can greatly improve a library's efficiency in this important area of library housekeeping.

Rationale for the Automation of the Acquisitions Function

- Reduced drudgery and error-proneness.
- Information sharing.
- Management Information reports.
- Status of ordered material.
- Accuracy.
- Tracking.
- Optimization of staff time and effort.

Automation can improve the efficiency and reduce the redundancies of the information and work flows involved in acquisitions work.

Infrastructure for an Automated Acquisition System

The requisites and support structures for an automated acquisition system include :

- Access to external databases and sources of Information.

- On CD-ROMs.
- Via the internet.
- Via online search systems.
- Via online library catalogues.
- Via library networks, service providers.

Internal databases and files An Automated acquisition system requires access to several local files and databases. Some of these are an integral part of the acquisitions system and in fact are created with in the acquisitions system. The following internal files and databases are typically needed :

- Library's online catalogue.
- User/membership files.
- Currency and exchange rate files.
- Authority files.
- In-process file.
- Order history file.
- Invoice data file.
- Financial data file.
- Vendor data file.

In Automated acquisition system, the above files are created and updated by the modules in automated acquisition system.

An Automated acquisitions system could be broken down into several sub-systems based on the discrete functions that are required to be performed. A typical automated acquisitions system will have the following functional sub-systems :

- Request Processing.
- Order data entry and updating.
- Order production and transmission.
- Received items processing.
- Claims.

- Accessioning.
- Physical preparation.
- Financial records, budgeting and reporting.
- Search and retrieval.

Management information reporting several sub-systems exist in an automated library system. The integration is extremely tight, and these sub-systems constantly exchange data. The acquisition sub-system in integrated library automation software should have interfaces to the following sub-systems :

- Cataloguing -must permit searching of the catalogue and downloading of catalogue data into the acquisitions systems files online public access.
- Catalogue must allow users to query acquisitions files, via the OPAC.
- Circulation system: Access to circulation statistics and interlibrary loan records, to enable such requests as additional copies of a publication.

4

Open Access Resources

"Right now, we have to manually search the library for information on topics for a project. It takes time and often it doesn't work. The e-library will allow you to get information within seconds".

—*Times of India*

Open Access

Open Access literature is free online for anyone, anywhere to read, download and use, providing that the author is properly cited. To be fully open access, literature must be freely available as soon as it is published. If not before. Open Access holds promise to remove both price and permission barriers to the scientific communication by using internet. Open Access is an obvious choice for works that authors have traditionally given way, such as scholarly, peer reviewed journal articles, the focus the open access movement. Open access makes sense for other materials too, such as government documents, thesis and conference proceedings.

Definition

Open Access is World Wide movements where in full-text scholarly article are completely free and unrestricted to all users to read, copy, download and distribute over the World Wide Web. [Directory of Open Access Journals (DOAJ).]

Budapest Open Access Initiative (BOAI) while there are multiple definitions and favours of open access. Open access basically calls for scholarly publications to be made freely available to libraries ad end users. It still stands as the most important definition of open access. The key passage from BOAI is: The literature that should be freely accessible online is that which scholars give to the world without expectation of payment. Primarily, this category encompasses their peer-reviewed journal articles, but it also includes any unreviewed preprints that they might wish to put online for comment or to alert colleagues to important research findings. There are many degrees and kinds of wider and easier access to this literature by "Open access" to this literature, we mean its free availability on the public internet, permitting any users to read, download, copy distribute, print, search or link to the full texts of these articles, crawl them for indexing pass them as data to software or use them for any other lawful purpose, without financial legal, or technical barriers other than those inseparable from gaining access to the internet itself. The only constraint on reproduction and distribution and the only role for copyright in this domain, should be to give authors control over the integrity of their work and the right to be properly acknowledged and cited.

Open Access is not Synonymous with Universal Access

Even after OA has been achieved, at least four kinds of access barrier might remain in place :

- *Filtering and censorship barriers.* Many schools, employers and governments want to limit what you can see.
- *Language barriers.* Most online literature is in English or just one language and machine translation is very weak.
- *Handicap access barriers.* Mostly web sites are not yet as accessible to handicapped users as they should be.
- *Connectivity barriers.* The digital divide keeps billions of people, including millions of serious scholars, offline.

Even if we want to remove these four additional barriers there is no reason to hold off using the term "open access" until we've succeeded. Removing price and permission barriers is a significant plateau other recognizing with a special name.

There are many business models compatible with OA, i.e. many ways to pay the bills so that readers can each the content without charge. Models that work well in some fields and nations may not work as well in others. No one claims that one size fits all.

There are many differences among the disciplines that affect the funding of OA. We should not expect OA to make progress in all disciplines at the same rate, any more than we should expect it to make progress in all countries at the same rate. Most of the progress and debate is taking place I the STM fields (Science, Technology, and Medicine) but OA is just as feasible and useful in the humanities.

New OA business, models are evolving and old ones are being tested and revised all the time. There is a lot of room for creativity in finding ways to pay the cost of a peer-reviewed OA journal or a generation purpose OA repository and we're far from having exhausted our cleverness and imagination.

- *OA is not a kind of license.* There are many licenses compatible with OA, i.e. many ways to remove permission barriers for users and let them know what they may and many not do with the content.
- *OA is not a kind of content.* Every kind of digital content can be OA, from texts and data to software, audio, video and multi-media. The OA movement focuses on peer-reviewed research articles and their preprints. While most of these are just text, a growing number integrate text with images, data and executable code. OA can also apply to non-scholarly content, like music, movies and novels. Eve if these is not the focus of most OA activist.
- OA serves the interest of many groups.
- *Authors*: OA gives them a worldwide audience than that of any subscription-based journal. No matter how prestigious or popular and demonstrably increases the visibility and impact of their work.

- *Readers*: OA gives them barrier-free access to the literature they need for their research, unconstrained by the budgets of the libraries where they may have access privileges. OA increases reader research and retrieval power. OA also gives barrier-free access to the software they use in their research. Free online literature is free online data for software that facilitates full text searching. Indexing mining summarizing, translating, querying, linking recommending, altering, "mash-ups" and other forms of processing and analysis.
- *Teachers and students*: OA puts rich and poor on an equal footing for these key resources ad eliminates the need for payments or permission to reproduce and distribute content.
- *Libraries*: OA solves the pricing crisis for scholarly journals. It also solves what I've called the permission crisis. OA also serves library interests in other indirect ways. Librarians want to help users find the information they need regardless of the budget-enforced limits on the library's own collection, Academic librarians want to help faculty increase their audience an impact and help the university raise its research profile.
- *Universities*: OA increase the visibility of their faculty and research, reduced their expenses for journals and advances their mission to share knowledge.
- *Journals and Publishers*: OA makes their articles more visible, discoverable, retrievable and useful. If a journal is OA, then it can use this superior visibility to attract submissions and advertising not to mention readers and citations. If a journal permits OA through post print arching, then it has an edge in attracting authors over journals that do not permit post print archiving. Of course subscription–based journals and their publishers have countervailing interests as well and often resist or oppose OA. But it oversimplified the situation to think that all their interests pull against OA.

- *Funding Agencies* : OA increases the return on their investment in research, making the results of the funded research more widely available, more discoverable, and more useful. When funding agencies disburse public funds, OA helps in a second way as well, by providing fundamental fairness to taxpayers or public access to the results of publicly funded research.
- *Governments* : As funders of research, governments benefit from OA in all the ways that funding agencies do. OA also promotes democracy by sharing non-classified government information as widely as possible.
- *Citizens* : OA gives them access to peer-reviewed research most of which is unavailable in public libraries and gives them access to the research for which they have already paid through their taxes. But even those with no interest in reading this literature for them will benefit indirectly because researchers will benefit directly. OA accelerates not only research but the translation of research into new medicines. Useful technologies, solved problems, and informed decisions that benefit everyone.
- *Open Access Initiatives* : Few Organizations, which are promoting Access Initiative among the publisher, institution and researcher. They are encouraging more and more publishers mostly learned societies to join the cause for providing free access to the scholarly literature.

Features of Open Access

- Open Access literature is not free to produce and publish, but is less expensive to produce than conventionally published literature ad also less expensive than priced online only literature.
- As long as the full text is OA, price add-ons are compatible with OA. If the enhancements are costly to

provide the producers have to charge accordingly. For some OA journals, priced add-ons take care of part of the revenue.

- OA is a kind of access, not business model, license or content.
- Copyright holders have to give their consent or owning license or permission statements along with their work.
- The important feature is that the bills are not paid by the readers and hence there are no access barriers.
- OA is compatible with copyright laws, peer-reviews, preservation, career advancements and indexing etc.
- OA project is a constructive programme and not destructive. It does not aim at putting non-OA journals or publishers out of business.

Types of Open Access

At this stage it is important to distinguish several dimensions of the issue: OA can be delivered in two ways :

- 'Green' the author can self archive at the time of submission of the publication (the green route) whether the publication is grey literature (usually internal non-peer-reviewed), a peer-reviewed journal publication, a peer-reviewed conference proceedings paper or a monograph.
- 'Gold' the author institution can pay a fee to the publisher at publication time, the publisher thereafter making the material available free at the point of access (the 'gold' route). The two are not, of course, incompatible and can co-exit.

The 'green' route makes publications availability freely in parallel with any publication system but it is not itself publishing. The 'gold' route is one example of electronic publishing. At present it is much more common to have non-OA electronic access to publications in a publisher's database for a subscription fee.

The second dimension to be distinguished is the timing and quality aspect, preprints are pre-peer-review articles, post prints are post-peer-reviewed ad post-publication articles while e-prints can be either but in electronic forum.

A third dimension is white/grey literature. White literature is peer-reviewed published articles while grey is preprints or internal 'know-how' material. Of course there are usually many interesting relationships between grey and white articles.

Today several companies world web have committed to supporting and developing open source software for libraries. They offer everything from hosting and installation to support and development services. With these new options, libraries don't need an IT staff to deploy software or steer development of new features.

Best Practices

- In order to promote the open access agenda, best practices should be shared with other Indian libraries and could include the following points.
- Show value to authors: Many authors need to provide a list of publication assessment purpose. Preparing publication lists and author web pages using open archives software can help convince authors of its wide applicability and the increased visibility it provides. Prolific authors can be specifically targeted.
- Provide access statistics, preferably at the document level. Uniform metrics should be adopted for all repositories.
- Get support from the top. Where top levels of administration support self archiving, institutional repositories have flourished.
- Create public opinion for mandating deposits. A recent statement at the special session on open access at the 93rd Indian Science Congress calling for mandatory.
- Deposit of research papers institutional repositories was targeted at funding agencies. The accompanying FAQ provided an explanation of open access.

- Increase training opportunities among staff by holding workshops and providing education on open access. This is already being done to good effect but needs to be more widespread by targeting universities and research laboratories.
- Provide better visibility by registering repositories with open access registers such as ROAR, Open DOAR and federated search services such as OAIster. (OAIster is a union catalog of millions of records representing open access resources).

Open Access Resources: Journals, self archived articles and search tools.

Open Access Resources

Budapest Open Access Initiative: http://www.soros.org/openaccess/

Open Access News: http://www.earlham.edu/~peters/fos/fosblog.html

elFL Open Access Program: http://www.elfl.net/services/services_open.html

Directory of Open Access Journals : http://www.doaj.org/

Directory of Open Access Repositories: http://www.opendoar.org/

SPARC (Scholarly Publishing and Academic Research Coalition): http://www/arl.org/sparc/about/index.html

Bioline International: http://www.bioline.org.br/

Public Knowledge Open Access Project: http://www.publicknowledge.orf/issues/openacess

CERN Workshop on Innovation in Scholarly Communications (OA 14): http://oai4.web.cern.ch/OA14/ (presentation abstracts ad streaming of presentations very informative)

JOISC Briefing Paper on Open Access: http://www.jisc.ac.uk/uploaded_documents/JISC-BP-OpenAccess-V1-fial.pdf

Public Library of Science: www.plos.org

BiMed Central: http://www.biomedcentral.com

Hindawai Publishing: http://www.hindawi.com

E Prints: http://www.eprints.org/

DSpace: http://www.dspace.org/

Resources for Librarians in Developing Countries:

1. Scholarly Resources- Freely Accessible Full Text Journals

A. Full Text Journals

1. Open Access/Almost–Open-Access on line Journals (any Country)

(a) Directory of Open Access Journals (DOAJ) http: //www.doaj.org.

This service covers free, full text, quality controlled scientific and scholarly journals. We aim to cover all subjects and languages. There are now 5787 journals in the directory. Currently 2467 journals are searchable at article level. Around five lakhs articles are included in the DOAJ service.

(b) African Journals on Line (AJOL) http://www.ajol.info

Current Awareness from tables of contents and abstracts. Some full text online. Print subscriptions to individual journals (subscription details online). Document Delivery through photocopy (sent by airmail), fax and email.

AJOL-funded document delivery (free) to low income countries. AJOL-subsidized document delivery ($9.00 per article to pay) to middle income.

(c) Bioline International http://www.bioline.org.br/journals

Bioline International is a pioneer in the provision of open access to peer-reviewed bioscience journals published in developing countries. These journals contain timely research on public health, international development, tropical medicine, food and nutritional security and biodiversity that would not otherwise be readily available to researchers in the developed world, or even within the country of publication. Bioline is not a publisher, but an aggregator that provides a free platform for journals who wish to participate in the global open access movement.

(d) Electronic Journals Library http://rzblx1.uni_regesburg.de/ezeit/index.phtml?bibid= AAAA&colors=7&lang=en

University Library Regensburg offers the "Electronic Journals Library" which contains 25,000 titles of which over 10,5500 journals can be read free of charge.

(e) High wire (Standford University) http://highwire.standford. edu/list/freeart.dtl/

High wire facilitates access to over 1.1. Million full text scholarly articles on medical biomedical topics. Most journal title covered includes back issues order than 12-24 months.

(f) Scholarly Journals distributed via the World Wide Web (university of Houston Libraries)http://info.lib.uh.edu.wj/webjour.html

Provides links to established web-based scholarly journals that offer access to English Language articles. No user registration or fees required.

(g) British Library for Development studies. http://blds.ids.ac.uk/blds/elibrary/ej-list.html

Click on List only free internet editions

(h) ideas at RePEc http://ideas.repec.org/search.html

B. JOURNALS ACCESSIBLE FREELY FOR SELECTED DEVELOPING COUNTRIES-SOME MAY REQUIRE REGISTRATION

1. Electronic Information for Libraries http;?/www.eifl.net

ElFL.net is an independent foundation that strives to lead, negotiate, support and advocate for the wide availability of electronic resources by library users in transition and developing countries. Its main focus is on negotiating affordable subscriptions on a multi country consortia basis, while supporting the enhancement pf emerging national library consortia in member countries.

2. AGORA- Access to Global Online Research in Agriculture: http://www.aginternetwork.org/en/journals.php

AGORA provides free access to more than 500 journals from major scientific publishers in the fields of food, agriculture, and environment science and related social sciences. AGORA is available to students and researchers in qualifying not–for–profit institutions in eligible developing countries. For more information contact agora@fao.org.

3. HINARI- Health Internet work Access to Research Initiative http://extranet.who.int/hinari/en/journals.php

The Health Internet work Access to Research Initiative (HINARI) provides free or very low cost online access to the major journals in biomedical and related social sciences local, non-profit institutions in developing countries.

4. OARE–Online Access to Research in the Environment http://www.springer.com/sgw/cda/frontpage/0,11855,4-198-2-172659-0,00.html

OARE is being developed under the sponsorship of the United Nations Environment Programme with infrastructure provided by Yale University. OARE is scheduled to be launched in January 2007.

5. High wire Press (Standford University) http://highwire.standford.edu/list/freeart.dtl

High wire provides a list of journals offering free online access to developing economies. Individual publishers use the World Bank's list of low income economies of the determining access. You do not need to register for this service as high wire software automatically detects the country you are connecting from and grants access accordingly.

6. OXFORD Journals–Developing Countries offer http://www.oxfordjournals.org/access_purchase/developing_countries.html

Oxford University press offers developing countries free (or greatly reduced rate access to may of our journals via our Developing Countries Online Collection offer. The offer via the

International Network for the Availability of Scientific Publications (INASP) for established not-for-profit educational institutes from qualifying countries and provides access to an Online Collection of Journals.

7. Global Development Network (GDN) Free Journal Access Portal http://ww.gdnet.org/middle.php?oid=245

GDN has linked policy research institutes from 11 regions and more than 100 countries. GDN offers a range of Journals services to address the difficulty faced by many researchers in the global south in accessing journals articles to support their research.

8. TEEAL–The Essential Electronic Agricultural Library http://www.teeal.org/about.html

TEEAL is a full text and bibliographic CD-ROM library of more than 140 of the world's most important scientific journals in the field of agriculture. It is available well below cost to more than 100 of the lowest-income food-deficit countries.

C. DIRECTORIES/INDEXES FOR DETERMINING PUBLISHER OPEN ACCESS STATUS

1. Index of Author-Archiving Status

Romeo lists the status of publisher copyright policies and author-arching policies of academic journals. Indicating by a color scheme which publishers allow authors to archive preprints and post-prints. Journals are classified by color as green, blue, yellow and white levels. http://www.sherpa.ac.uk/romeo.php?all=yes

2. Institutional Repositories

Most of the research activities in an institution are carried through and funded by the research programmers and grants of that institution. Institutional repositories aim to provide online the outcome of these research activities in scholarly publications in their institutions/server to enhance wider access to their publications. With its library as the focal point, institutional repositories are expected to bring online at the research activates of the institution for open access and with further collaboration with other such repositories to provide broader access to research. Institutional repositories are envisaged to centralize preserve and make accessible an institution's intellectual capital and at the same time they will ideally from a part of global system of distributed, interoperable repositories that provide the foundation for a new disaggregated model of scholarly publishing. Above all institutional repositories aim to offer considerable benefit to the institution, its participant's ad users by projecting a institution's intellectual visibility.

Both these Open access models of scholarly publication are gaining momentum. It is estimated that over three thousand open access journals are now available online. So far more than three hundred institutions around the globe have successfully implemented the institutional repository mode. There are various funding modes and publishing models available for these initiatives. The successful acceptance of the initiatives in the academic clearly shows that in future to scholarly publication will be available free ad open to the research community. All these positive responses suggest that the transition from the existing publishing model to a free and open one has begun.

A. FULL TEXT OPEN ACCESS REPOSITORIES

1. Directory of Open Access Repositories (Open to DOAR) http://ww.opendoar.org

Open DOAR lists the wide variety of institutional and subject-based Open Access research archives and repositories which have grown up around the world.

2. OAIsterhttp://oastr.umdl.umich.edu/cgi/bib/bib-idx?= oaister;page=simple

OAIster is a collection of freely available, previously difficult to access, academically oriented full-text resources searchable without restriction. OAIster includes over 7 million records from over 600 institutions worldwide.

3. ARC–A Cross Archive Search Service: http://arc.cs.odu.edu

Arc is an experiment research service of Digital Library Research group at Old Dominion University. ATC searches across over 178 International repositories (http:// arc.cs.odu.edu:8080/aooai/admi.jsp) through a unified search interface.

4. e-Prints-UK project http://eprint-k.rdn.ac.uk/search/ ?view=advanced

e-Prints-UK aims to provide national, discipline-focused searching for access of journal articles, technical reports and web pages in electronic institutional archives of 30 selected UK universities and colleges.

5. Bielefeld Academic Search Engine (BASE) http:// basesearch.net/index.php?i=a

BASE is the multi-disciplinary search engine to scholarly internet resources at Bielefeld University. BASE complements the current Meta search system for catalogues and databases of the Bielefeld Digital Library by allowing searches to be limited by type of document, including scholarly full text archives, digital repositories and preprint servers available on the World Wide Web.

B. FULL TEXT INSTITUTIONAL RSPOSITORIES FOCUSING ON DEVELOPMENT

1. FAO Corporate Documents Repository/FAO http:// www.fao.org.documents

The repository provides full text access to publications articles and meeting documents produced by the FAO.

2. Development experience database/ U.S. AID http:// www.dec.org

Provides access to abstract and the full text documents from USAID, including Reports, development project documents, and citations of documents held by USAID information Centres.

3. World Bank-"Documents and Reports" Database http:// www-wds.worldbank.org

Provides access to al publicly available World Bank operational documents (Project documents, analytical advisory work and evaluation) formal and information research papers, and most World Bank publications. Includes 15000 full text documents.

4. Development Gateway/Development Gateway Fdn http://www.developmentgatway.org

Promotes knowledge sharing by providing access to full text documents across a wide range of development topics. Also includes 398 country Gateway Portals serving local development information needs.

5. Eldis Gateway to Development Information Inst of Dev Studies http://www.eldis.org

Over 16,000 full text abstracted development oriented documents are available from Eldis. Documents are of "strategic, policy or practical interest" for development practitioners based in both the North and the South.

6. UN Best practices Database http://www.bestpractices.org

Includes descriptions of over 2,150 award-winning solutions to common social economic and environment problems in over 140 developing and developed countries. Searchable by country, Scale (global, national, regional, village etc.) and by subject category. Best practices is a joint product UN-HABITAT and The Together Foundation and are supported in part by the Dubai Municipality, the Best Practices Partners and the Government UK. Coverage 1996 present.

7. Projects and Operations – World Bank http://www.world bank.org/projects

Search thru projects project documents and analytical–and-advisory work of the World Bank. An advance search feature is available. The data base is also brows able by region, country/area, theme or sector.

C. FREE STATISTICAL DATA SOURCES FOCUSING ON DEVELOPMENT TOPICS

1. World Development Indicators (text Display)/World Bank http://www/worldbank.org.data

Query database selection here: http://devdata.world bank.org/data-query

World development indicators (WDI) are the World Bank's Annual compilation of data about development. The 2005 WDI includes more than 800 indicators in 83 tables organized in 6 sections. World View people environment economy, states ad markets and global links. Data are shown in 152 economics with populations of more than million and 14 country groups, plus selected indicators for 56 other smaller economies limited access to statistical database. Full access available via subscription only.

2. FAOSTAT Databse /Food q and Agriculture Organization http://faostat.fao.org

Multilingual statistical databases containing over 1 million time series records covering international statistics in the areas of production, trade, food, balance sheets fertilizer and pesticides, land use ad irrigation, forest products, fishery products, population, agricultural machinery, ad food ad shipments.

3. LABORSTADatabase/International Labor Organization http://www/lbaorsta.ilo.org

Contains yearly statistics of employment, unemployment hours of work, wages, labor cost, consumer price indices, occupational injuries, strikes and lockouts on over 200 countries (data since 1956). Monthly statistics of employment and unemployment, hours of work, wages, consumer price indices data since 1976) and economically active population estimates and projections1950 - 2010.

4. Creditor Reporting System (CRS)/OECD and World bank http://www.oecd.org/dac

Contains data on Official Development Assistance (ODA) Official Aid (OA) and other lending to developing countries and countries in transition as collected by members of the Development Assistance Committee the World Bank, ad the regional financial institutions. The system is sponsored jointly by the OECD and the World Bank operated by the OECD.

5. DAC Online /OECD http://www.oecd.org/dc/stats/idsonlie

DAC measures the flows of aid and other financial

resources to aid recipients. Collected annually from the members of the OECD's Development Assistance Committee these statistics are broken down by major category of expenditure capital projects, budget and balance of payments support, food and other commodity aid, technical cooperation and emergency relief.

6. UN Monthly Bulletin of Statistics /United Nations http://unstats.u.org/unsd/mbs

Includes currently monthly economic statistics for most countries and areas of the World. The statistics are obtained by from official sources in the various countries, except where otherwise stated in the notes to the tables. Updated monthly.

7. UNSTS UN Common Database/ United Nations http://unstas.un.org/unsd/cdb

Draws selectively on statistics from throughout the UN system, covering all countries areas and over 300 series from more than 30 specialized international data sources. Time series data is generally available from 1970 or 1980. Many series are disaggregated to show underlying distributors. The source includes comprehensive footnotes and meta-information on source, definitions and frequency of updates and provides technical definitions and standard verbatim from their original sources. Users may view data compile graphs calculate derived measures and export data.

D. FREE CITATION DATABASES

1. Online Journals requiring Subscriptions/Global Development Network http://www.gdnet.org/middle.php/oid=247#online

The site lists databases providing full text access to online journals, mostly by subscription. Other services, such as citation searching email alerts on new journals abstracts and table of contents alerts are usually freely available.

2. JOLIS Library Catalog/ World Bank/IMF http://jolis.worldbankimflib.org/e-nljolis.hym

The Jolis Library Catalog is the catalog of the IMF/World

Bank Library Network. The Catalog, which contains over 1 million items, includes references to a wide variety of development related materials from hundreds of different publishers. The catalog also includes references and links to many published IMF and World Bank materials.

3. Global Jolis Library Catalog/World Bank http://jolis.world bankimflib.org/e-nlglobaljolis.htm

Global Jolis is the Library catalog for World Bank Country Office PIC (Public Information Center)/Libraries. It includes materials in most country offices around the world. The catalog includes references to books, journal articles, working papers conference proceedings, technical reports, electronic resources, and country-specific reports from local government agencies non governmental organizations, speech collections of local language and indigenous knowledge materials.

4. ERIC/US Department of Education (English, French, Spanish) http://www.eric.ed.gov

ERIC includes references to journal articles and on-journal material covering aspects of education. The database contains over 1.1 million citations from 1966 to the present. More than 107,000 full texts, non-journal documents (issued 1943–2004) are available.

5. FAOBIB- FAO Library Catalog-/Food and Agriculture Organization http://www4.fao.org/faobib

FAOBIB is a multilingual, on-line catalogue of documents and publications produced by FAO since 1945, books added to the library collections since 1976 and serials held in the FAO library. Full text links are now provided for all documents which are available electronic format.

6. AGricola/U.S. Department of Agriculture http://agricola. nal.usda.gov

A Comprehensive source of bibliographic citations covering US agricultural and life sciences information. Agricola contains over 3,500,000 citations to journal articles monographs, theses, patents, software, audio-visual materials and technical reports related to all aspects of agriculture.

Coverage is from 1970 to the present with monthly updates. Some citation in French.

7. UNESBIB- UNRSCO Documents Database http://unesdoc.unesco.org/ulis

UNESBIB includes over 100,000 citations for books, articles and UNESCO publications, some with full text links. Languages included are: English, French, Spanish, Arabic and Russian.

8. Red Latinoamericana de Documentation e Informacion en Education (REDUC) (Spanish only) http://www.reduc.cl/homereduc.nsf/?Open

REDUC es un system cooperative de recopilacio, procesamineto y diseminacion de documentos relevantes enel campo de la education en la region de America Latin y el Carbie.

9. PubMed http://www.ncbi.nlm.nih.gov/entrez

PubMed provides access to over 11 million citations from the US National Library of Medicine and other related databases. Links to selected online journals some freely available are also included. Updated monthly. Covers 1960s to present. Some citations are in French, Portuguese or Spanish.

10. Popline http://db.jhuccp.org/popinform/basic.html

Popline is the world's largest bibliographic database on population, family planning and related health. Citations also cover sexually transmitted diseases including HIV/AIDS, reproductive health, and law and policy issues. The database includes abstracts of journal articles, monographs, technical reports, and unpublished works. Updated twice per month. Some Citations in French, Spanish or Portuguese.

11. Science Direct http://www.sciecedirect.com

A Collection of over 1,000 journal title citations with links to the full text by subscription only. Science Direct focuses predominantly on science, technology, and medicine, but mathematics, economics and other disciplines are represented. Some citations in French.

12. UNBISnet/UN Dag Hammarskjold Library http://unbisnet.un.org

Catalogue of United Nations documents and publications indexed by the UN Dag Hammarskjold Library and the Library of the UN office at Geneva. Also includes are commercial publications another non-Un sources held in the collection of the Dag Hammarskjold Library. The Coverage of UNBISnet is from 1979 onwards, however, older documents are being added to the catalogue on a regular basis as a result of retrospective conversion. UNBISnet also provides instant access to a growing number of full text resources in the six official languages of the UN, including resolutions adopted by the General Assembly, the Economic and Social Council ad the Security Council from1946 onward.

12. Google Scholar http://www/google.com/scholar

Google Scholar facilitates citation searching of scholarly literature including peer-reviewed papers, theses, books, preprints, abstracts and technical reports from a broad range of research areas.

SCHOLARLY JOURNAL DOCUMENT DELIVERY SUPPORT SERVICES FOR DEVELOPING COUNTRIES

A. Electronic Journals Delivery Service (eJDS) Programme http://www.ejds.org

The electronic Journals Delivery Service (eJDS) Programme is geared to facilitate free access to current scientific literature. The Goal is to distribute individual scientific articles via email to scientists in institutions in Third World countries that do not have access to sufficient band with to download material from the Internet in a timely manner and/or can not afford the connection.

B. African Journals OnLine (AJOL) http://www.ajol.info

AJOL offers a free document delivery service for developing countries. There is a document delivery fee for requestors outside of developing countries.

C. Electronic Supply of Academic Publications to and from Universities in developing regions (ESAP) http://fluc.org/iaup/esap

A Project of the International Association of University Presidents (IAUP) in cooperation with the International Federation of Catholic Universities (IFCU), SAP aims to set up a sustainable electronic document delivery systems for scholarly publications between universities in the North and the South as well as on a South-South basis, and thus assist in the supply of academic publications to as well as from the developing world.

D. A Library in your Letterbox: The GDN/BLDS Document Delivery Service http://www.gdnet.org/online_services/journals/gdn_journal_services/document_delivery/index.html

Accessing the latest development knowledge is a key challenge for many researchers in developing and transition countries. Recognizing these challenges, the Global Development Network and the British Library of Development Studies (VBLDS) have teamed up to bring GDN/BLDS Document Delivery service to meet the information needs of research institute in the South.

E. International Network for the Availability of Scientific Publications (INASP)/Programme for the Enhancement of Research Information (PER) http://www.inasp.info/peri

This network provides access to Scientific and scholarly information through electronic means. It includes more than 10,700 full-text online journals current awareness databases, and document delivery of major scientific, technical, and medical, social science, and humanities materials from a wide range of sources. For more information contact inasp@inasp.info

F. Free for All http://www.geocities.com/wfb_2/freeforall.html.

Free for all is an international collaboration of libraries whose mission is to provide underserved nations with health science journals articles for free.

OPEN (FREE) COURSEWARE

MIT Open Courseware http://ocw.mit.edu

MIT OCW is a large-scale, web-based electronic publishing initiative whose goals are to provide free, searchable access to MIT's course materials for educators, students and self-learners around the world ad extend the reach and impact of MIT OCW ad the "Open courseware" concept.

SOFIA- Sharing of Free Intellectual Assets http://sofia.fhda.edu

As of February, 2006 content for eight courses was available online freely thru the Sofia open content initiative. The Sofia project is an open content initiative launched by the Foothill-De Anza Community college District with external funding support.

JHSPH Open Courseware http://ocw.jhsph.edu

The Johns Hopkins Bloomberg School of Public Health's Open Courseware (OCW) project provides access to content of the School's most popular courses. Includes undergraduate and graduate subjects available on the web, free of charge, to any user anywhere in the world.

TUFTS Open Courseware http://ocw.tufts.edu

Tufts Open courseware includes course content in life sciences, with a multidisciplinary approach, an international perspective, and an underlying ethic of service.

Utah State University Open Courseware http://ocw.usu.edu/About/index_html/ECDocument_ viewUSU

OCW is a free and open educational resource for faculty, students and self-learners throughout Utah and around the world. OCW support's USU's mission to serve the public through leaning, discovery and engagement.

Open Learning Initiative at Carnegia Mellon http://www.cmu.edu/oli/overview/index.html

A Collection of "cognitive informed" openly available and free online courses are course materials that enact instructions for a course in an online information.

Information Management Resource Kit (FAO) http://www.fao.org/imark

The Information Management Resource Kit (IMARK) is a partnership-based e-learning initiative to train individuals and support institutions and networks world-wide in the effective management of agricultural information IMARK consists of a suite of distance learning resources, tools and communities on information management. IMARK is being spearheaded by FAO in collaboration with over 30 partner and contributing organizations.

Concept of E-resource

An E-resource is defined as a resource which requires computer access or any electronic product that delivers a collection of data, be it text referring to full text bases, electronic journals, image collections, other multimedia products and numerical, graphical or time based, as commercially available title that has been published with an aim to being marketed. These may be delivered on CD-ROM, on tape, via Internet and so on.

Benefits of Open Access E-Resources

The benefits of Open Access e-resources are:

- It is freely available and simultaneous accessible at anytime and anywhere by any users.
- It removes price barriers like subscription fee, licensing fee, pay-per-view fee and permission barriers such as copyright and licensing restrictions.
- It supports full text searching with various options such a keyword, phrase, Boolean, Proximity etc.
- There is no need to worry about the stole, misplace, and reserved to check out of the documents.
- It support e-learning through global access of information, collaboration and exchange of ideas.
- It promotes digital materials and enhanced preservation of knowledge for present and future generation.

- It is easier to update and produce new form of information.
- It reduced cost of conventional libraries like building, professional staff and maintenance and preservation of reading materials.

SUBJECT GATEWAYS

Subject gateways allow you to browse subject lists of good quality ad evaluated subject resources.

Bubl Information Services (http://bubl.ac.uk/)

It is a UK-based interactive information service which provides links to over 12,000 internet resources in wide range of subject areas. It used the DDC system as the primary organization structure for its catalogue of internet resources.

Cogprints http://cogprints.org/

It is an electronic archive for self archive papers in any area of psychology, neuroscience, linguistics, computer science philosophy biology medicine anthropology as well as any other portions the physical social and mathematical sciences that are pertinent to the study of cognition.

DMOZ : Open Directory Project : http://www.dmoz.org

It is the largest most comprehensive human-edited directory of the web. Namely arts, business, computers games, health, home kids and teens news recreation, reference, regional sciences, shopping, society, sports worlds etc. It is constructed and maintained by a vast global community of volunteer editors.

E-print Network http://www.osti.gov/eprints/

It provides access to 5 million electronic preprints available from 32,000 websites and databases that deal with scientific and technical disciplines namely, physics, chemistry, biology, biotechnology, geosciences materials science, nuclear sciences, engineering energy research mathematics environmental sciences, computer and information technologies etc.

Infomine http://infomine.ucr.edu

It is a virtual library of Internet resources relevant to faculty, student and research staff at the university level and contains useful internet resources such as databases, electronic journals, electronic books bulletin mailing list online library card catalogs articles directories of researchers and many use types of information.

Intute http://www.intute.ac.uk

It provides a trusted source of selected high quality international information for students academics, researchers and practitioners in Science and Technology, Arts and Humanities. Social Sciences, Health and Life Sciences.

Math guide http://www.mathguide.de/

It is an Internet-based subject gateway to scholarly relevant information in mathematics. In it resources are described and evaluated with a set of Dublin Core metadata.

Pinakes : A Subject Launched http://www/hw.ac.uk/libwww/irn/pinkes/pinakes.html.

It is a compilation of Internet resources, which links to the major subject gateways, such as AERADE, AHDS, ChemDex, ELDIS, FMO, gem etc. and multi subject gateways, such as Infomine, Intute, Bulb Link, DMOZ, etc.

Renardus : http://renardus.sub.uni-goettingen.de/

It provides a source of selected high quality Internet resources for teaching, learning and researching in higher education in Europe.

SocioSite http://www.sociosite.net/

It is a project based at the faculty of Social Sciences at the University of Amsterdam. It is designed to get access to information and resources which are relevant for sociologists and other social scientists. The main intention is to provide a comprehensive listing of all sociology resources on the Internet.

Voice of the Shuttle http:// vos.ucsb.ed

It provides a structured and briefly annotated guide to online resources in the humanities and associated disciplines, such as anthropology, archaeology, architecture, etc.

WWW Virtual Library http://vlib.og/

It is the oldest catalogue of the Web, started by Tim Berners-Lee in 1991 at CERN in Geneva. It indexes cover a broad range of subject areas, such as agriculture, law, education, etc. Each entry within a subject area links to the appropriate internet resource and is accompanied by a brief description and a relevancy ranking.

Yenza http://www.nf.ac.za/yenza/

It is a guide to using the Internet for research and teaching in the Social sciences and Humanities and it also provides links to online resources relating to specific disciplines.

Barriers to Open Access

- *Loss of Publisher income*: The major objection to 'green' self-archiving comes from publisher's ad learned societies (many of which depend on subscriptions to their publications) who fear that 'green' OA threats their business viability. To date there is no evidence that 'green, archiving harms the business model of publishing. There is evidence that 'green' archiving increases utilization, citation and impact of a publication. While the major commercial publishers provide the additional value-added services that could offset the impact of OA on current business models, the impact on learned societies may require now business models to be developed.
- *Copyright*: Copyright agreements between authors and publishers may inhibit the "green" route. However to date between 80 and 90% of the publication channels allow green author deposit although some insist on an embargo period before the publication is available for OA. In contrast some publishers of journals of which nature is the most well known do not demand copyright from the author but merely a license to publish leaving copyright with the author or their institution.

Advantages of Open Access

The major OA is research impact the available e-article is likely to have more accesses citation and impact. However there are additional advantages.

5

Role of Internet and Web Technologies

Role of Internet and Web Technologies in providing novel Information Resources and promoting Information Literacy.

People looking for Information on a subject matter, especially for academic or research purposes were generally confined to the traditional print resources like books, journals and monographs available in their libraries. Increasing use of Information Technology and the rapid growth of internet have led to vast improvements in the way information is generated, stored and retrieved. Emerging technologies have now opened up new avenues for information like online databases, e-journals, subject portals, blogs etc. Digital resources and e-content now form a major chunk of available information. The changing role of libraries now includes developing awareness among the academic community regarding these new information sources. Today's education system also needs to be revamped to accommodate the emerging technologies and educators must now inculcate new information seeking skills among their students to make them Information literate. This article seeks to examine the various ways in which information is now available online. It also elaborates on various new technologies being used to improve information literacy among students in particular.

Introduction

This is organized into two sections. The first section attempts at understanding how internet and World Wide Web have led to the emergence of novel information resources like online journals, blogs, etc. The second section tries to enlist the various technologies being used to effectively transfer information thereby promoting information literacy. Taken in its entirety, it tries to understand the impact of internet and web technologies on information retrieval and usage from two diverse standpoints.

Information Literacy has been defined by the American Library Association as "A set of abilities requiring an individual to recognize when information is needed, and have the ability to locate, evaluate and use effectively the needed information". Information literacy is a life long skill that extends across disciplines. It allows users greater access to a wide range of resources and gives them the critical ability to examine the credibility and usefulness of available information. The first step towards gaining information literacy is the ability to locate diverse sources of information. This paper first discusses the various sources of information available online.

Looking for Information on the Internet

Until recently, people had to depend upon books, journals, monographs (books written on a single subject in a scholarly manner by a specialist) and conference proceedings for literature review or subject queries. Many additional information sources are now available like open access journals, open access and institutional databases, creative commons resources, wikis, page flakes, blogs, user forums, social networking sites etc. Search engines are now the most favoured/most used medium for looking for information. However, actually gathering relevant information from search engine results is a highly arduous task. Users need to be aware of the various kinds of search engines available and also hone their search techniques to make effective use of these search engines.

Search Engines

A search engine is an online tool designed to search for information on the World Wide Web. The search results are usually presented as a listing of web pages or images or other types of files. Google, Microsoft bing, Yahoo and Ask are among the most commonly used search engines.

Some subject specific search engines are also available that can be used when searching for information related to a particular subject. However, while some of these search engines provide access to free content, most of them require users to pay one-time/subscription fee in order to access content. The following is a listing of the most commonly referred search engines for specific subject needs.

Law students can refer to the following specific search engines :

Manupatra http://www.manupatra.com

Supreme Court – India http://www.judis.nic.in

Lexis Nexis (American Law) www.lexisnexis.com

Westlaw www.WestLaw.com

Medical students can refer to the following search engines:

Indian Medicine http://www.indianmedicalsites.in/

GoPubMed Knowledge-based search engine for biomedical texts www.gopubmed.com

Bioinformatic Harvester A bioinformatics Meta search engine http://harvester.fzk.de/harvester/

www.webMD.com for general medical queries.

Search engines on various other categories are also available. Sites like moster.com, naukri.com, careerbuilder.com are used in searching for jobs. Google news, yahoo news, lexis nexis can be used for news related searches. There are also specific web search engines to look for maps, multi media content, prices and product reviews, blog searches etc.

Important Subject Specific Search Engines for Research Purposes

The search engines listed above are mostly useful for general or simple subject queries. However, if the users want results that are credible, scholarly and have been peer reviewed, they can make use of some specific subject search engines.

Google Scholar http://scholar.google.co.in/

Google Scholar is a freely-accessible Web search engine that indexes the full text of scholarly literature across an array of publishing formats and disciplines. Google Scholar allows users to search for digital or physical copies of articles, whether online or in libraries. Google Scholar is relatively quick and easy to use. Searches will be done from full-text journal articles, technical reports, preprints, theses, books, and other documents, including selected Web pages that are deemed to be scholarly. Because most of Google Scholar's search results link directly to commercial journal articles, a majority of the time users will only be able to access a brief summary of the articles topics, and small amounts of important information regarding the article, and possibly will have to pay a fee to access the entire article.

Scirus from Elsevier http://www.scirus.com/

Scirus is the most comprehensive science-specific search engine available on the Internet, linking to more than 167 million indexed scientific pages and documents. With Scirus we can search through a variety of sources, such as Medline, Science Direct, Biomed Central, preprint servers, patents and web sites relevant for our research.

CiteSeerX http://citeseerx.ist.psu.edu/

CiteSeer^x is a scientific literature digital library and search engine that focuses primarily on the literature in computer and information science. CiteSeer^x provides resources such as algorithms, data, metadata, services, techniques, and software that can be used to promote other digital libraries.

getCITED http://www.getcited.org/

getCITED is an online, member-controlled academic database, directory and discussion forum. Its contents are entered and edited by members of the academic community. In addition to the books and articles accessible with other databases, book chapters, conference papers, working papers, reports, papers in conference proceedings and other such research outlets can all be entered and then searched for within getCITED.

Techniques for Searching

Search engines search on the web by making use of the search terms (Keywords) typed in by the user. Users can make use of a few techniques that will simplify their search process and return relevant results.

Keywords

The most important factor in doing successful online searches is selecting good search terms. Using alternate terms or synonyms also results in better results. The search should be very generic at first and then users can search for specific information once again from the results retrieved by the general search.

Boolean Operators

Users can make use of Boolean operators like AND and OR along with their keywords to get better results.

(i) AND narrows the search. All the words entered as search terms must be found.

(ii) OR broadens the search. Any of the words from the search terms will be found.

For ex.: A Google search for Information AND literacy retrieved around 7,970,000 results, while the same search for Information OR literacy returned 26,200,000 results. Using the OR keyword led to a 150% increase in amount of information retrieved.

Phrase Searching

When the Keywords being entered as search terms consist of multiple words, users can go in for phrase searching. All the search terms are enclosed in a set of quotation marks and this forces the search engine to look only for sources where all the terms appear together as a phrase.

For e.g. the search term "Information Literacy" returned 1,140,000 results while only the keywords Information Literacy returned over 7,970,000 results. Phrase searching narrowed down the search results tremendously.

Truncation

Searches for variations on a word by adding a special character at the end of the root word. Users can make use of wild cards like? or * to search for related terms.

E.g.: Searching for litera* will return links to sources that contain words like litera, literal, literate, literacy etc.

Nesting

This technique combines various searches like phrase searching along with Boolean operators. Users can make use of braces and Boolean operators to narrow down their searches. For e.g. the search term ("Information Literacy" AND "Information Technology") retrieved only 234,000 results while the same terms without nesting, Information Literacy and Information Technology will return over 3, 720,000 results.

In spite of the wide number of results being generated by search engines, they are not always sufficient for academic purposes. The kind of information retrieved through search engines usually suffers from a lack of credibility; timeliness ad generally leads to information overload. Also, search engines usually access only a limited, public portion of the World Wide Web. A large number of subject specific gateways and subject portals are now available where users can find credible information that has been reviewed.

Subject Gateways/ Subject Portals / Subject Directories

These websites provide links to web sites on a particular

subject area. Most are designed to help students and academicians find high quality web sites for their studies and often include descriptions and evaluations of the web sites. Some of them also provide Search facilities, links to related sites and resources such as Electronic Journals (Open Access or subscription based), Discussion Groups, Mailing lists and many specialized user facilities required for users of specific disciplines.Resources on subject gateways are generally selected by editorial review process.

Subject portals offer access to resources and services in a unified manner. Subject directories are collections of websites sorted by an editor into subject groupings e.g. Yahoo.

The best example of a subject gateway/portal is at http://www.intute.ac.uk/ which covers Science and Technology, Arts and Humanities, Social Sciences and Health and Life Sciences.

Listing of Important Subject Gateways Found Online

Library and Information Science http://bubl.ac.uk

Agriculture http://www.agrigate.edu.au

Engineering http://www.intute.ac.uk/engineering

Education http://www.edna.edu.au/edna/go

Chemistry http://metachem.ch.adfa.edu.au

Health and Medicine www.intute.ac.uk/medicine

Humanities http://www.intute.ac.uk/artsandhumanities (formerly Humbl)

Life sciences (Biome)

Physical sciences (psigate)

Reference sciences (rdn),

Social sciences (Sosig) are all available at www.intute.ac.uk

Cancer (Information from National Cancer Institute-U.S.) http://www.cancer.gov/

Genome http://www.nature.com/omics/index.html

Computer Science - http://liinwww.ira.uka.de/bibliography/index.html

Listing of multi subject gateways that provide resources on a large number of subjects

http://bubl.ac.uk/link/

Bulletin Board for Libraries - A general gateway to all major academic subject resources for UK higher education, including other university library catalogues and electronic journals.

Http://infomine.ucr.edu/

A Web resource featuring well organized access to important university level research and educational tools on the Internet.

http://www.intute.ac.uk/

A free online multi-subject gateway providing users with access to the best web resources for education and research. This service is created by a network of UK universities and partners. Subject specialists select and evaluate the websites in the database and also provide high quality descriptions of the resources.

http://www.ipl.org

(Librarians internet index - A searchable, annotated subject directory of Internet resources selected and evaluated by librarians for their usefulness to users)

http://www.vlib.org.uk/

(WWW Virtual Library - A catalogue of quality web resources covering a broad range of subjects)

http://www.about.com/education/index.htm

http://www.dmoz.org/ (Open Directory project)

Yahoo (UK) Yahoo (US) A combined search engine and subject gateway offering access to Web resources in a wide range of different subject areas.

http://www.hw.ac.uk/libWWW/irn/pinakes/pinakes.html

Pinakes Subject gateway that provides access to Internet resources, by linking to the major subject gateways. Includes links to resources on art, chemistry, libraries, education and other topics.

http://www.library.usyd.edu.au/hussarr

A subject gateway to information resources in the study of French humanities and social studies (excluding law). Searching is by author, title, subject and keyword.

Online Databases (Free/Subscription)

Some of the most useful online sources are databases with the full-text of articles from thousands of newspapers, magazines, and journals. Some of these can be accessed freely or through an institution's library website. Some require one-time or subscription payments in order to access full text of articles. These databases usually contain thousands of articles on a wide variety of topics. Some Subject specific databases are also available that provide reference material on a particular subject area. Needed information can be located in various journal collections.

N-list Website

The national library and information services infrastructure for scholarly content provides online access to students from colleges across India. An initiative of Ministry of Human Resources Development (MHRD), this project by UGC INFLIBNET (University Grants Commission – Information Library Network) provides for cross-subscription to e-resources and access to selected e-resources to students, researchers and faculty from colleges and other beneficiary institutions. The authorized users from colleges can now access e-resources and download articles required by theme.

An authorized user from colleges registered under NLIST programme, will have access to the following e-resources. E-Mail: college@inflibnet.ac.in

E-Journals (Fulltext)

American Institute of Physics (18 titles)

American Physical Society (10 titles)

Annual Reviews (33 titles)

Cambridge University Press (224 titles)

Economic and Political Weekly (EPW) (1 title)

Indian Journals (150 titles)

Institute of Physics (46 titles)

Oxford University Press (206 titles)

Royal Society of Chemistry (29 titles)

H. W. Wilson (1420 titles)

E-Books

E- brary (45000+ titles)

Oxford Scholarship (902 titles)

Net Library (936 titles)

MyiLibrary-McGraw Hill (1308 titles)

Academic Search™ Premier

http://search.ebscohost.com/

Designed specifically for academic institutions, this is the world's largest scholarly, multi-disciplinary full text database containing full text for nearly 4,650 serials, including more than 3,600 peer-reviewed publications. In addition to the full text, this database offers indexing and abstracts for more than 8,200 journals in the collection.

Examples of titles offered in Academic Search Premier include: American Historical Review, British Journal of Psychology, Early American Literature, English Language Notes, Family Relations, International Journal of Psychology, Journal for the Scientific Study of Religion, Journal of Politics, Journal of Psychology, Journal of Social Psychology, Library Journal, Social Forces, Sociological Review, Theological Studies, Women's Studies, etc.

http://info.scopus.com/

Scopus is a database of abstracts and citations for scholarly journal articles. It covers nearly 18,000 titles from more than 5,000 international publishers, including coverage of 16,500 peer-reviewed journals in the scientific, technical, and medical and social sciences (including arts and humanities) field. It is owned by Elsevier and is provided on the Web for subscribers.

http://www.sciencedirect.com/

Science Direct is a full-text scientific database offering journal articles and book chapters from more than 2,500 peer-reviewed journals and more than 11,000 books. There are currently more than 9.5 million articles.

http://agricola.nal.usda.gov/

The most comprehensive source of bibliographic citations covering US agricultural and life sciences information. AGRICOLA contains over 3.7 million citations to journal articles, monographs, theses, patents, software, audio-visual materials, and technical reports related to agriculture.

http://isiwebofknowledge.com/

ISI Web of Knowledge is an online academic database provided by Thomson Scientifics' Institute for Scientific Information. It provides access to many databases and other resources: Web of Science (including Science Citation Index (SCI), Social Sciences Citation Index (SSCI), Arts & Humanities Citation Index (A&HCI), Biological Abstracts, Index Chemicus, and Current Chemical Reactions, covering about 8,700 leading journals in science, technology, social sciences, arts, and humanities, ISI Proceedings, Current Contents Connect, Medline, ISI Essential Science Indicators, Journal Citation Reports (two editions: Science and Social Sciences), in-cites, Science Watch, ISI HighlyCited.com, Index to Organism Names, and Biology Browser. Use of ISI Web of Knowledge is licensed to institutions such as universities and the research departments of large corporations.

Examples of some other commonly used databases are scientific databases like Chemical Abstracts and Entrez, and databases of images, such as ARTstor.

Online Journals

The Internet has revolutionized the production of, and access to, academic journals (Hendler 2007), with their contents available online via services subscribed to by academic libraries. Various kinds of journals are available for use, like (i) *E -journals* - a journal in electronic format. Some e-journals are electronic versions of printed publications, whereas others are available only in electronic format. (ii) *Academic journal* - a journal intended principally for students and staff doing serious study in universities or other academic institutions. (iii) *Peer-reviewed journal* - A journal whose articles have been read by other scholars before publication and judged by them to be of a sufficiently high standard to be included in the journal. (iv) Open access journals are scholarly journals that are available online to the reader without financial, legal, or technical barriers. Some are subsidized, and some require payment on behalf of the author.

Accessing Online Journals

http://www.doaj.org/

The Directory of Open Access Journals (DOAJ) lists open access journals, that is, scientific and scholarly journals that meet high quality standards by exercising peer review or editorial quality control and are free to all from the time of publication.

http://www.openj-gate.com/

Open J-Gate is one of the world's largest database of Open Access Journals.

http://www.ncbi.nlm.nih.gov/pubmed/

PubMed comprises more than 19 million citations for biomedical articles from MEDLINE and life science journals. Provides indexed citations to medical, nursing, dental, veterinary and healthcare articles.

http://www.eric.ed.gov/ERICWebPortal

ERIC provides unlimited access to more than 1.3 million bibliographic records of journal articles and other education-related materials. ERIC users include education researchers, teachers, librarians, administrators, education policy-makers, instructors and students in teacher-preparation programs, parents, the media and business communities, and the general public. The user community conducts more than eight ERIC indexes education journals, the majority of which are peer-reviewed.

http://www.jstor.org/

JSTOR (short for *Journal Storage*) is an online system for archiving academic journals, founded in 1995. It provides full-text searches of digitized back issues of several hundred well-known journals, dating back to 1665 in the case of the *Philosophical Transactions*.

http://www.ingentaconnect.com/

INGENTA CONNECT provides free use of comprehensive collections of academic and professional publications. Online articles from over 30000 publications are available. Abstracts are free; full text is available by subscription or pay-per-view

Online journals provided by publishers:

http://www.springer.com/online+journals+archive

http://www.interscience.wiley.com

Online Catalogs

Almost all reputed colleges, universities and academic institutions provide access to multiple sources like books, microfilms, print journals, e-journals, Audio and Video resources in the form of CD's, DVD's etc. Users should ideally begin their information quest by checking out the OPAC's of their respective institutions. An OPAC (or Online Public Access Catalogue) is a computerised networked catalogue which shows what a library possesses. It can be searched by various search methods and can display the location of the material. Accessing library catalogs of reputed institutions provides access to many online databases and journals subscribed to by that library.

Some websites accessible through OPAC's of Indian universities:

Indcat http://indcat.inflibnet.ac.in/

Online Union Catalogue of Indian Universities is unified Online Library Catalogues of books, theses and journals available in major university libraries in India. The union database contains bibliographic description, location and holdings information for books, journals and theses in all subject areas available in more than 121 university libraries across the country.

Digital library of Osmania University, Hyderabad -

http://dli.iiit.ac.in/

OPAC of Univ of Hyd Library:

http://igmlnet.uohyd.ernet.in:8000/

UGC-INFONET Digital Library Consortium, A Gateway to India's Academic and Research Community

http://www.ugcinfonet.jccc.in/

Open Source and other Resources

Wikis

A page or collection of web pages designed to enable anyone who accesses it to contribute or modify content, using a simplified markup language. Wikis are often used to create collaborative websites and to power community websites. The collaborative encyclopedia Wikipedia is one of the best-known wikis.

http://www.wikipedia.org/,http://en.wikipedia.org/wiki/Wikibooks , http://commons.wikimedia.org/wiki/Main_Page

Free e-books

Large collections of completely free and downloadable electronic books are available for free use at 1. Project Gutenberg

http://www.gutenberg.org/wiki/Main_Page

Archive.org http://www.archive.org/index.php.

Archives: Archives are documents created and/or accumulated by institutions, businesses or even individuals in the course of their daily life and work and retained in perpetuity. The term is also used to refer to the building and/or organization which keep them. Ex: web.archive.org.

Newspaper Archives: News paper archives easy way to search through historical news. Ex. Google news

http://news.google.co.in, http://ibiblio.org

Open Source Applications: Dspace Open source software enables open sharing of content that spans organizations, continents and time.

http://www.dspace.org

Grey Literature: Consists of Reports, patents, conference papers, government documents, newsletters, bulletins etc. that are not readily available through commercial channels.

Apart from knowledge regarding various online resources, it is also necessary to understand the various technologies being made available online/offline in order to make good use of these resources. The next section of this paper attempts to explain the various novel ways in which educators are making use of various tools in order to make their students information literate in the true sense of the word.

Utilizing Emerging Technologies

Using Software Packages and Hardware Tools

Information Literacy is essentially a combination of various skills that include tool literacy (ability to use IT tools like software packages), resource literacy (ability to locate resources), research literacy (ability to use IT tools for research purposes), publishing literacy (ability to format and publish research) and emerging technology literacy (ability to understand and make use of the continually emerging innovations in information technology - Shapiro and Hughes). Tools like Microsoft office make it easy for teachers to present their concepts in a variety of ways through power point shows, excel spread sheets, word documents etc. Notes can be easily prepared and shared through use of packages like Microsoft Word and WordPerfect. Tools like Microsoft PowerPoint help in creation of captivating custom slide shows. Packages like Excel and Access help in number crunching, statistical analysis and database management. Similarly, a large number of software packages are available for specific disciplines like CAD/CAM for civil and automotive engineering., simulation software etc. Students must be encouraged to be conversant with some basic hardware/software as fluency in Information Technology is an essential component of Information Literacy.

Utilizing Multi-media Content

Teachers now have access to rich multi-media content that they can make use of in improving the information literacy levels of their students. Multi-media content can be easily incorporated by teachers into their regular class room teaching to make their classes more informative and interesting. Websites like hulu, arkive.org and youtube.com and slidecast.net are of good help in this regard. Teachers can use these websites to search for videos on their subject areas or create their own videos and upload them.

For e.g. A search for videos related to Information Literacy on youtube.com will return many interesting and educative videos on this topic. Many videos by highly esteemed faculty members of world class institutions are also available for free viewing either on sites like you tube or on their individual institutional websites. The open course ware project of MIT allows users to freely access lecture notes, exams, and videos.

Similarly, many audio resources are also freely available online. Recordings of free courses from institutes like Stanford and Yale, free audio lessons for learning foreign languages, many classic books and novels in audio format are all available for free downloading. By being aware of these multiple sources, students can now search for audio/video information also. Slide casts are a similar kind of content that are increasingly being offered. A number of slide casts are also available online which are a combination of slide shows with audio content. Teachers can incorporate these new forms of information into their regular curriculum and help students with creating and utilizing diverse content.

Technologies Made Available by Web 2.0

The advent of Web 2.0 has given rise to web applications that facilitate interactive information sharing, interoperability, and collaboration on the World Wide Web. Examples of Web 2.0 include web-based communities, hosted services, web applications, social-networking sites, video-sharing sites, wikis, blogs, mashups and folksonomies. A Web 2.0 site allows its users to interact with other users or to change website content, in contrast to non-interactive websites where users are limited to the passive viewing of information that is provided to them. This has had a dramatic impact on how and where teachers/ students look for information. Some of the technologies made possible by use of web 2.0 can be used by teachers as part of their regular curriculum in the following ways.

Search Engines, User Forums and Online Communities

Students searching for information on any particular issue had to depend either on their teachers or on any books/ journals that were available in their local libraries. Thanks to the prevalence of computers and internet, students can now make use of the many search engines and user forums that are available on the net. Commercial search engines like Google and yahoo provide links to a large number of resources. Teachers can also search for additional resources to aid in their teaching through commercial search engines like google.com or subject specific search engines like scirus.com

User forums or message boards are online discussion sites where people can post messages and comment on other's posts. Teachers can make use of these user forums to improve their knowledge base or direct their students to forums that can help with their student's queries. Most user forums on any specific subject have hundreds of queries already answered. So in most cases, students don't even need to wait for responses but can browse through replies already posted. User forums also enable students to access and exchange ideas with their peers across the world. For e.g. various forums are available on information literacy where users can discuss new ideas, problems, provide suggestions etc.

Teachers can also make use of the vast number of user groups/online communities to effectively communicate with their students. Most groups feature extensive information regarding their specific subject areas and this knowledge base can be expanded with newer queries and responses. Teacher-student groups can also create their own communities through websites like yahoo or Google and use these forums for discussing new ideas and to exchange information.

Online Tools

Teachers can also make radical changes to their instructional methodologies by using online tools like web blackboard, webct, webex etc. While some of these tools need to be bought by the educational institutions for a fee, some allow users to make use of free trial versions. These tools essentially help a teacher to conduct most of his/her teaching online. Teachers can allow their respective course students to access their blackboard account through a user/password combination. Once the students login to their class account, they can all access the various resources posted online by their teacher for that particular course. This could include notes in the form of word documents, slides, handouts or even previously recorded lectures. Links to a variety of outside resources like online journals, expert blogs, tests and quizzes etc. can also be included. Discussion boards are provided where all students can post their queries/comments/assignments. These tools can be used in sync with VoIP software like skype to make voice calls. This allows all the students to interact and share their ideas on a common platform but with the added comfort of doing it from their own homes at their desired time.

Various websites allow teachers to conduct real time seminars (webinars) with students located at different geographical locations by using a combination of discussion boards and video conferencing. Students are no longer confined by physical boundaries and can interact with their peers/teachers/experts across continents in their search for valuable information. "Knowledge webs" are thus enabling students to have distributed access to experts, archival resources and shared investigations.

Blogging, Networking and Social Bookmarks

Micro blogging, social networking and book marking are examples of other recent IT trends that are extremely popular with the younger generation. Educators can make innovative use of these features to improve their student's information literacy capabilities. A vast number of people across professions are maintaining blogs or web logs on a wide range of subjects. These blogs allow teachers and students to access a wide variety of information. For e.g. A web search for blogs on information literacy will return a huge number of highly informative blogs being maintained by information literacy enthusiasts all across the world. Teachers can share a list of their favourite blogs that contain relevant and useful subject information with their students or even maintain their own blogs/ twitter accounts. Students can be directed to these blogs to enhance their knowledge base.

Social book marking can also be used to maintain lists of all available online resources for future references. Social book marking is a method for Internet users to share, organize, search, and manage bookmarks of web resources. Unlike file sharing, the resources themselves aren't shared, merely bookmarks that reference them. In a social book marking system, users save links to web pages that they want to remember and/or share. These bookmarks are usually public, and can be saved privately, shared only with specified people or groups, shared only inside certain networks. Book marking sites like delicious and digg are of great help in organizing resource references and greatly reduce the time being spent on retrieval of information that was previously located.

Micro blogging is a form of multi-media blogging that allows users to send brief text updates or micromedia such as photos or audio clips and publish them, either to be viewed by anyone or by a restricted group which can be chosen by the user. These messages can be submitted by a variety of means, including text messaging, instant messaging, E-mail, digital audio or the web. Sites likeTwitter allow users to post their thoughts in a short and concise form within short intervals of time and share it with their friends or followers. Teachers and educational institutions/libraries can effectively use micro blogging as a means of disseminating information regarding class schedules, assignments, due dates etc.

Mobile Applications, SMS, RSS Feeds and Podcasts

Most teachers/students now have access to mobile devices that provide a host of built in applications. Searching for information or exchanging it has become even simpler and quicker. Having a wi-fi enabled mobile device allows teachers and students to search for information from a vast repertoire of online databases almost instantaneously. Students can configure their computers or mobile devices to receive RSS feeds/Podcasts from websites/blogs/communities. RSS is a format for delivering regularly changing web content. These feeds automatically download content as it is created freeing us from the task of searching for any new content posted. For ex. students can receive RSS feeds from a blog maintained by a teacher. This way, anytime the teacher updates the content on his/her site, students automatically receive it and can view it immediately.

Pod casting is the automatic distribution of mp3s via RSS/ XML files. In simpler terms, a pod cast is a pre-recorded audio program that's posted to a website and can be downloaded automatically, stored and viewed any time. Educative Podcasts on a variety of subjects are being offered by many websites which can be received by students through their mobiles.

Short Messaging Services (SMSes) are another way of disseminating information quickly on a real time basis. SMS is an acronym standing for Short Message Service. It is commonly referred to as text messaging or "texting" as well. SMS is a method by which messages can be sent to a cell phone via another cell phone, a computer connected to the Internet, a regular land line, or a handheld device such as a Blackberry. Many college and library websites are now making use of RSS feeds and SMS services to inform their patrons of any new updates or availability of new resources.

Many other online tools are also available like tools for creating lesson plans, tests and quizzes, year planners and schedules, screen recording and screen sharing, online photo editing, online document editing etc. Teachers and class rooms should leverage these technological developments by incorporating them into everyday teaching so that access to information can be transformed into useful knowledge.

To be considered information literate in today's world, one must be fully conversant with using diverse sources like search engines, online portals and subscription databases. Users should be trained to have the ability to 1. Know where to look for information based on purpose i.e. general searches/ subject specific queries through gateways. 2. They must be able to locate necessary information from the vast collections of online journals available and be able to access them. 3. Be fully cognizant of the diverse resources being offered by libraries and make efficient use of these resources. Knowing where and how to look for information would be a great first step in making users truly information literate. The second step necessitates exposure to the various web technologies and tools and sufficiently training them to obtain necessary information. A person who is information literate should be able to survive the challenge of too much information understand how to harvest knowledge from a vast information reserve. The instructional paradigm being used by educators and traditional services being offered by libraries must be modified to accommodate the additional capabilities made possible by use of Information Technology.

Some Useful E-Resources

http://ir.inflibnet.ac.in/

http://etd.ncsi.iisc.ernet.in/

http://drtc.isibang.ac.in/DRTC/

http://dspace.library.iitb.ac.in/jspui/

http://www.dspace.org/institution/anwesan-snltr-by-cse-iit-kharagpur.html

http://dspace.nitrkl.ac.in/dspace/

http://dspace.mit.edu/

http://www.opendoar.org/countrylist.php

http://www.indiabix.com/

http://dspace.vidyanidhi.org.in:8080/dspace/

http://www.dspace.cam.ac.uk/

http://dspace.mona.uwi.edu/

http://eprints.cmfri.org.in/

http://eprints.rclis.org/

http://eprints.iisc.ernet.in/

http://www.eprints.org/

http://mdrf-eprints.in/

http://eprints.iari.res.in/

http://mdrf-eprints.in/

http://eprints.immt.res.in/

http://eprints.eemcs.utwente.nl/

http://www.osti.gov/eprints/

http://eprints.qut.edu.au/

http://www.maths-in-industry.org/miis/

http://www.orgprints.org/

http://eprints.aktors.org/

http://eprints.bham.ac.uk/

http://www.lib.unimelb.edu.au/eprints/

http://eprints.hec.gov.pk/

http://eprints.nmlindia.org/

http://eprints.utas.edu.au/

http://genesis2.jpl.nasa.gov

http://www.theassc.org

http://arxiv.org/

http://eprintweb.org/S/

http://www.nzdl.org/gsdlmod?a=p&p=about&c=gsarch

6

Role of Libraries in New Digital Era

Introduction

With the advances in information and communication technologies the libraries are now changing to what may be called virtual or digital libraries. It has affected significantly the nature of delivery of library resources and services.

The Information Communication Technology led initiatives in the form of e-learning. The e-learning market is booming all over the world and is predicted to follow an upward swing with more and more institutions, organizations and individuals implementing and adapting to this mode. The power of e-learning lies in its potential to provide the right information to the right people at the right time at right place. The users having access to the internet and those who have adopted to learning through computers have shown their preference for e-learning over print. The traditional concept of organization, bibliographic description and dissemination of information are to be fine tuned to the new environment by the library and information professionals. So the library professionals working in the present environment have to face challenges. Hence it becomes important for the clients to develop skills in new technology so that they can identify, evaluate the relevant information effectively.

From leaf to clay tables, from manuscripts to microfilms, from printed documents to CDROMs and online electronic resources, libraries and information centers have always been in the business of facilitating information to its diversified categories of users. The library professionals are always in fore front in devising, developing and using various tools and technologies to facilitate content-based information to its end users. The internet has completely transformed the traditional method of processing information from collection to communication. In Modern era information in the digital form is rapidly replacing the traditional printed counterparts, resulting in increased computer skills, processing tools and fast communication network connectivity.

Evolution of Libraries

Paper Library	Automated library	Electronic library
Collections= Paper	collections=paper	collections=digital
Bibliographic	Bibliographic	Bibliographic
Control=Paper	control=electronic	control=digital

1995	1995-date
Traditional Library Vs Virtual Library	Modern Library
Traditional Library Internet	Modern Library
User goes to library	Library goes to the users
OPAC	Web based OPAC
Documents (Books, Journals etc.)	E-Resources (E-Books, E-Journals etc.)
Cataloguing and Indexing, Classification	Search Engines and Metadata
Circulation (issues and returns)	Access direct with internet facility
Resource sharing	Consortium

Tools for Research Scholars

Previously it is said that research starts in the library and ends in the library. Now-a-days it starts in the internet and ends in the internet. The internet can be very useful to researchers. To navigate the internet librarians and researchers will find search engines very helpful tools. A search engine is an online tool designed to search for information on the World Wide Web. World Wide Web search engine is defined as retrieval services, consisting of a database or databases describing mainly resources available on the WWW. Users need to be aware of the various kinds of search engines and can effectively make use of them.

Electronic Information Sources

The amazing technological advancements have opened new horizons for information creation, duplication, storage, access, distribution and presentation. The pace at which information sources are being produced and converted into electronic form is marvellous. Digitization of Information is resulting in access to an unbelievable volume of information. Obviously, information from electronic sources cannot be accessed in the same manner as printed sources were consulted previously. Adequate knowledge about computers and retrieval techniques are desirable to effectively search these electronic information sources.

Electronic Publishing

The main products of electronic publishing are electronic books, electronic journals, electronic databases and electronic articles.

Electronic books: CD_ROM (Compact disk only memory), CDROM Books, CDROM journals, D.V.D. (Distal Versatile Disk), Optical Disks+.

Electronic Database

They are of two types: off-line systems and online systems. In off-line systems, the information is stored in mainly CDROMs whereas in online systems the information is stored in the main frame to be distributed and made available at the local computers through networks like the internet. The multimedia information sources are available in the following formats :

CDROMs/ DVDs

Videodiscs (VD)

Laser Disks (LD)

Audio and Video Cassettes

Web

Databases on servers

Digital Video

Impact of Electronic Publishing on Libraries

The era of electronic publishing has brought a change in the nature and type of library services. Publishing through the network, especially internet has made the libraries more responsible towards their users. The impact of electronic publishing on libraries is in the following manner :

- Increased access to online catalogues and databases has changed the nature of library services to users.
- The notion of "Virtual Libraries" where users transparently access needed information.
- Regardless of location, depend on no-cost; unrestricted access to electronic information becomes possible.
- It is possible for the users to place their own interlibrary loan requests electronically at libraries world-wide, indifferent to the source of the needed item.
- As computer network interconnections and capabilities have increased, the concept of 'global village' has become a much more immediate day-to-day reality in libraries.
- Internet links provide remote users with significantly increased access to library systems.
- The user community greatly benefited due to the proactive, positive response by librarians to electronic environment.

- The users can employ internet to search remote online catalogues as easily as they can search their local catalogues.

Role of Librarian in New Environment

The revolution in ICT had brought an evolution in reference and information services. The impact of internet is playing a vital role in all the fields of Science and Technology and education and its learning techniques advanced research makes the librarian to depend on live and e-mail reference services. In order to adapt to the technological advances and transform in accordance with technology-driven information needs of users' information professionals need to update their knowledge and upgrade the skills for offering real time services to users. ICT fundamentals operating library software, trouble shooting, and website design constitute the job oriented skill, whereas user oriented skills comprise of networking, digitalization, e-sources and services, Information literacy promotion etc. Library professionals should cultivate the new skills to cope up with the present digital era. The Librarian should develop good communication skills, information research skills, technical skills and managerial skills. They should have the ability to reorganize the Library from time to time, to meet the different needs of the users. Proper induction highlighting the resources, services, products and the people who can render the information should be introduced to the Fresh users. High importance should be given to develop the professional and soft skills of the information personnel. Apart from traditional methods of training like sending people for relevant courses, seminars and on the job learning methods they should be imparted with technical trainings like installing and updating the necessary software for the Library, knowledge of security technologies like firewalls, authentication, access controls, security related and virus counter measures. Librarians need to get into the social networks and virtual research environments. They should make use of the opportunities they get to share their best practices with their peers/colleagues in industries/academic fraternity. They must communicate each other discussing about the recent trends in LIS profession and must tackle the hurdles they come across. Library managers should encourage team work and the people working in a team should get due recognition for their role in developing innovative services/ outlook for their Libraries. Personnel with good professional, technological and knowledge competencies would get an auspicious future in technological era.

In short the present library professionals should have the following Competencies

Competencies are the skills, technical knowledge and personal attributes that enable individuals to contribute positively to their organizations and the library and information profession.

- Actively pursues personal and professional growth through continuing education.
- Recognizes the nature of the library's patrons and community.
- Demonstrates a strong commitment to excellent customer service.
- Demonstrates knowledge of the library system and the library profession.
- Understands the social, political and economic context in which the library exists.
- Demonstrates knowledge of library and information science theory, information.
- Creation, organization and deliver.

Many authors believe that librarians have a strong future in the networked environment (Rapple, 1997). Despite many fatal forecasts about the demise of librarians, information professionals continue to do their job, adjusting it in the new information environment, facing more complex requests, patrons' expectations that keep on growing (Tenopir and Ennis, 2001). The point is that librarians need to be proactive and not passive in delivering new services connected to the networked and digital environment. Some authors also believe that "there is considerable potential for the librarians to become involved with the process of improving access to significant internet content", because of their experience with the management and classification of information resources (Sturges, 2001).

F.W. Lancaster, introducing a collection of essays under the title 'Libraries and the Future', observes that as we enter the 21st century, significant changes will occur in the way in which sources of information, inspiration and entertainment will be made available and these changes will have a major impact on the LIS professionals. Giving a wake up call to the LIS professionals, he emphasize that there is a need to develop leadership qualities, acceptance and keeping pace with the technology. Further, stresses that we should use technology as supplement to the traditional/manual methods.

As Salter, 2003 rightly puts, the qualities of a modern librarian should be in the following manner :

> "The LIS professionals are perhaps designated as Information Officers, Knowledge Workers, Information Scientists, Knowledge Manager etc. It is a professional who encompasses a set of standards and values that operate smoothly and seamlessly in a technology driven environment. It is a professional who has a clear understanding of and appreciation for the traditions of librarianship. It is a professional who is multifaceted and multitasked. It is a professional with the characteristics of willingness to change; varied experience in training and background; adaptability to a quickly changing environment; 'share ability' between disciplines; and commitment".

Digital technology is one of the greatest innovations of the 21st century. E-learning allows for efficient transfer of knowledge any where and anytime, regardless of subject matter. Information technology brings laurels to the present libraries. The most of the information is now available in digital format. Library collections are now slowly changing into digital format. The ever-ballooning nature of information poses a big problem for librarians. So no library can afford to procure all resources. Librarians are now in a position to find the new way of functioning. At the juncture it is very important to analyze cost effectiveness of 'Digital Information". The cost-effective analysis generally helps to find the possible alternative methods of operating systems with low cost and high efficiency.

7

Library Automation Over View

"As technology advances, it reverses the characteristics of every situation again and again. The age of automation is going to be the age of 'do it yourself.'"

—*Marshall McLuhan*

Review of Literature

Library and Information centers are constant pressure to meet the changing and increasing demands from users for specific, appropriate and nascent Information. Information technology has already influenced and influencing various sectors of society. Libraries are no exception when every sphere of work and activity is exploiting the advantages of IT, libraries are not afford to stick on to conventional practices. This chapter reviews the literature on impact of IT and computer applications in libraries published in various professional Journals. The main aim of this reviewing is to trace out the state-of-art of applications of IT in various library operations. The studies have been organized chronologically under different sub-headings for the purpose of reviewing.

Impact on Libraries (General)

Murthy (1997) describes about the scope of Information Technology and stated that Information technology covers areas which can be grouped into the broad disciplines of computer communications, the developments in management information systems like libraries, databases and networks both online and off-line and reprography and Mass Communications covering the technological used for presentation and dissemination of information.

Abdul Rashid (1998) describes a methodology for converting a traditional library into a modern information technology based library. The various steps involved in the changes taking over are discussed. The in-house method of conversion of library records into machine-readable form is advocated along with management of the system.

Circulation Control

Flexuer defines circulation as "the activity of the library which through personal contract and a system of records supplied to the reader with the material". Computers were first used for circulation control in U.S. in the early 1960's and in U.K. in late 1960's. The following articles present the status of automated circulation activities in libraries.

Ravichandra Rao (1988) did a study on circulation control system in Indian Scenario (1988). The following institutions have defined and developed computerized circulation control system in India. (a) Indian Institute of Petroleum, Dehradun (b) TIFR, Bombay (c) Reactor Research Center, Kalpakam (d) NAL, Bangalore , (e) HAL, Bangalore (f) IDL Chemicals Ltd., Hyderabad.

All these are using simple and elementary systems based on punched cards. But TIFR is using mark. Sense card. In 1991 IIMC (Indian Institute of Management), Ahmedabad made experiments on Online Circulation system. All these libraries serving to limited users.

Ashok Jambakar and Neelameghan (1991) described detailed account on system design and output features of automated circulation system, which is adopted in IIM, Ahmedabad. A prototype circulation control system "CIRC" has been developed by Choudary and Choudary (1992).

Rama Krishna Reddy and Sudarshan (1997) described about the computer programs developed for the purpose of document circulation, in NICMAP (National Information Center for Machine Tools and Production Engineering) library. But after procurement of a PC exclusively for the library, the programs are re-written using d-Base III+ Software.

Johneston (1998) discusses about the value of Internet to the library and Information Science by examining it role in 3 areas. The impact of academic and scholarly periodical publishing and the dissemination of information; the contribution to reference work: and the impact on recreational reading. It concludes that the internet will be useful in the publication and distribution of scholarly electronic periodicals and the problems requiring solutions, particularly those relating to Bibliographic description.

Palaniyandy and Ravichandra Rao (1992) discussed the importance and need of automation in circulation section and creation of various databases and how the programs to be executed.

Serials Acquisition Processing and Control System

A serial as defined by the ISDS "A publication issued to successive parts and intended to be continued indefinitely." The latest methods to bring for libraries under control takes to the help of the computer, which is considered many a panacea for various wills of library jobs including those of processing and controlling of periodicals and serials.

INSDOC, New Delhi has adopted in 1975 centralized acquisition program for the various CSIR Laboratories.

Balakrishna (1987) discusses above the task first tasks taken up as part of the computerization activities to create a database of current periodicals received in the library and information services. A number of computer programs ware written in order to process the database and generate the desired types of list of journals.

Information Storage and Retrieval

Colvin More coined the phrase "Information retrieval in 1950. He described it as searching and retrieval of information from storage according to specification by subject.

Gopinath (1987) presents a set of criteria involved in the design in the development of information retrieval system analyses the value of facet analysis technique in the knowledge representation process.

Usha Rani and Sewa Singh (1994) discuss the capabilities of computers and define some selected terms used in computerized information retrieval system. Explains the concept of user education and trace development of this concept at national/international level.

Sreelatha and Neelameghan (1995) described micro ISIS developed and distributed by UNESCO which is used widely especially in developing countries in the end-user design and development of databases. It has facilities for designing end-user interfaces using the CDS/ISIS Pascal Program language. Such interfaces enhance the user-friendliness of the software.

Classification and Cataloguing

Aruna (1998) describes the developments in stand-alone systems led libraries to use these systems and streamline their data processing operations. Apart from routine operations the libraries started developing bibliographic databases by in putting. The bibliographic details of the books available in the particular library. Now the scenario is that these databases are available on networks.

Fleck and Margaret (1998) examines the development of micro MARC integrated format. It was first developed as micro MARC came in 1984 to address the specific issues associated with describing and managing archival material by the university archives and historical collections. Now this MARC-based information storage and retrieval software has been expanded to accommodate all MARC formats. The author examines micro-MARC for integrated format version 1.2 and its data entry.

Information Services

Abstracting Services

The Abstracting Service is important links in the chain of communications between the originator of the information and the user. This abstract would normally be a rough presentation of the full text. Apart from feasibility reader accessibility of computer produced abstracts has also to be taken into consideration by various authors.

Neogi and Chadda (1990) claims that the computerization of Indian Science abstract will reduce the processing time and help bring out the final output on target. It contemplates the creation of machine-readable. And searchable national Database to Indian Scientific and Technical Literature.

Indexing Service

Narayanan Kutty and Abraham (1998) discusses the processing and automated indexing of microfiche documents provided by SRIM (Selected Research In Microfiche) service, module developed for the purpose using CDS/ISIS a software developed by UNESCO.

CAS/SDI

According to Patwarohn report (1985) the impact and use of information technologies is also seen in some special libraries. The principles and methods of machine based SDI services experiences.

Library Software

Krishnanda Hertala and others discusses (1996) about the Pascal interface with CDS/ISIS, an information storage and retrieval package produced and distributed by UNESCO is widely used in Europe and many developing countries. It supports most of the requirements for designing bibliographic textual databases. The CDS/ISIS Pascal programming facility can be used to create end-user interfaces for any specific additional requirements. The standard CDS/ISIS package does not provide for data validation with respect to sub-fields and to check weather any mandatory fields have been missed during data entry. This paper discusses the need for data validation and operation of CDS/ISIS databases. The Programs enable specification of mandatory field's validation of such fields and in advertent of sub-fields limits in the master records and obtaining online help about the use of interface programs.

Harinaryan (1997 brings out his experience, which is using LIBSYS for acquisition in the library of IGNOU. Libraries have three options for software acquisition. They are developing the software in house, processing customizable software. There is an increasing trend in adoption of commercial systems in libraries in India. LIBSYS commercially available integrated library housekeeping software is being used at IGNOU library.

The experience of the author in using the acquisition module of LIBSYS system is described under the heading verification and order record creation, order preparation and transmission receipt and check in claiming and cancellations invoicing and accessioning payments library book funds and salaries management information reports and statistics documentation and training and system report. This article not only focuses on the capabilities of the LIBSYS as far as its acquisition module is concerned but also highlights the lacuna observed in various functions of the system.

Haravu (1998) describes the feature of DELPHI-ISIS a new format end-user interface for CDS/ISIS Databases under windows 95/NT attempt to provide solutions to some of the problems faced by user with the standard DDS version of CDS/ISIS DELPHI-ISIS via GUI-based 32 bit applications and user Boland's Rapid Application Developments tools. Using the single document interface model (SDI). Information technology brings together in single window the entire search, browse, display, sorting printing and downloading functions user get concurrent access to search history, retrieved records dictionary of search terms and any terms. User can customize search output, and search two or more databases concurrently. Hyper text links enable selection of words/strings from a displayed record to formulate new search expression or modify one in use. The paper highlights the advantage and current limitations of DELPHI-ISIS and outlines intended future developments.

Library Information and Newtworks

Networking in Libraries

Networking is the linkage of working procedures for the exchange of information resources. Presently, the term "computer network" is used in place of "resource sharing" or cooperative systems. Resource sharing or networking is defined as a mode of operation, whereby information resources are shared by a number of participants having the same objectives in mind. Thus the user of one library can have his requirements fulfilled by another library if the local library fails to serve his needs. Some of the essential prerequisites for effective resource sharing include :

- Possession of shareable resources by the participating libraries;
- Willingness to share the resources;
- A planned mechanism of sharing;
- Precise understanding of the use and information potential of their respective collections;
- Common bibliographic access to the collections of the participating libraries.

Even libraries with good budgets or collections cannot have enough resources to be self-sufficient. In fact, interdependence has now become a way of life. In recent years we have witnessed the establishment of a great number of networks around the globe through which technology is utilized to facilitate a vast flow of information. This ultimately will enable and support applications which influence people's daily lives. The major factors which have created the need for networking include the rise in the cost of publications, a lack of funds and adequate manpower, and the geographical dislocations of libraries, *i.e.*, the fact that libraries are now located in remote and far–flung areas.

- The ultimate aim of networking is to achieve maximum results with minimum input. This is clearly consonant with the nature of our economy, in which capital is scarce. Networking is inevitable in all types of libraries, for it enables users to have access to the resources of many other libraries, in addition to their own The benefits which accrue from resource sharing are the following:

- Preparation of union catalogues;
- Preparation of the cataloguing data/catalogue cards for publications available in network libraries;
- Provision of bibliographies;
- Optimum utilization of rare collections;
- Cooperative exchange and distribution and storage of documents;
- Savings of both technical work and collections;
- Reduction in the cost of library services, in the long run;
- Above all, the provision of more materials at low cost and in less time.

Against all odds, India has made rapid strides in recent decades in the field of telecommunications via satellite and microwave links. Networking systems have been developing fast at local, state, national, regional and international levels all over the world since the 1980s. In order to keep pace with the world, the Indian government is developing its own networking systems via NICNET. Surprisingly, the government does not consider libraries to have a high priority. Thus, libraries have to plan their acquisitions keeping in mind the resources available in other libraries in the area, so that they can get the maximum number of books and publications which are not available in their vicinity. In the past few years, considerable progress has taken place in the planning and building of library and information networks. As a result, four major networks — INFLIBNET, DELNET, CALIBNET, BONET— have started functioning in libraries.

Inflibnet

INFLIBNET started functioning in 1988 with the aim of optimizing the utilization of resources and avoiding their duplication. INFLIBNET has proposed to network 200 universities, 7,200 colleges, and over 200 research organizations attached to scientific, agricultural, medical, social science and defence organizations. It would be a multiservice network aiming at providing catalogue-based services, access to databases and document supply services, and facilities for computer mediating. In the initial plan, the thrust is on linking the most remote and needy universities with rich and rare collections. In the later phases, other university libraries would be linked. These are some of the salient features of INFLIBNET:

- It shall contribute to pooling, sharing and optimizing resources.
- It shall modernize libraries and information centers.
- It shall have multiple function/service networks.
- It is estimated that in India, ₹ 150 crores per annum are being spent towards books and journals by libraries concerned with higher education, and yet the needs of the users cannot be met fully.
- It shall help the libraries to develop unique collections.
- It shall help in avoiding duplication in procuring costly books and journals.
- It shall help to establish instant contact with other libraries in the country.
- It shall help libraries to improve their efficiency.
- It shall operate at different levels — national, regional, sectoral and local.
- It will help libraries to update their catalogues, and all catalogues will be aggregated from the bottom up, *i.e.,* from college and department to university library and regional centre.
- Users will be served mainly at local levels such as college, department, university and R&D institutions.
- There will be a national centre for managing, overseeing, and coordinating affairs of the networks,

and four regional centres (north, south, west, and east) to maintain union catalogues of library holdings.

- At the sectoral level, UGC information centres are included, and these centres will acquire, create, and access retrospective and current bibliographical databases.

Communication Hierarchy of INFLIBNET

INFLIBNET is designed to operate at four different levels—national, regional, sectoral and local. The networking will be hierarchical in nature. A college library will be linked to a university library, which in turn will be linked to the Regional Centre and Sectoral Information Centres. Multilateral communication is possible, but only via the Central hub in New Delhi. The whole network is envisaged as a star configuration except in the large cities where libraries are to be linked by terrestrial Local Area Network (LAN). According to L.J. Haravu, Library Manager, International Crop Research Institute of Semi-Arid Tropics (ICRISAT), multilateral communication in most cases will be only for message transfer and not for database access. Such an approach is all right in the beginning, but at a later stage when more and more libraries will become proficient at using computers, libraries will begin to look for more and more autonomy in computer use, database development, and access to external databases. Such a phenomenon has occurred in the West. It remains to be seen how INFLIBNET will cope with this situation.

DELNET

DELNET began its operation with the introduction of e-mail service in 1991, and has since then linked 35 libraries in the Delhi area. Participating libraries are using different software, such as CDS/ISIS, LIBSYS, CFS, DELMS, MINISIS, and dbase-LC-MARC. These libraries have saved a considerable amount by avoiding duplication of journals and other reading materials. The DELNET database has become one of the major bibliographic databases in India.

The network adopted Common Communication Format (CCF), developed by UNESCO, and AACR-2 as the code for developing cataloguing. H.K. Kaul, Director of DELNET, says that DELNET saved ₹ 25 lakhs in 1991, ₹ 25 lakhs again in 1992, and nearly . ₹ 50 lakhs in 1993 through rationalization of foreign periodicals. NISSAT and the Department of Electronics played a vital role by providing free modems and e-mail software. More libraries in Delhi are joining DELNET and making inquiries about online access to the Union catalogue. The British Council and NIC have helped DELNET in providing necessary assistance. The *DELNET Newsletter*, first published in January 1994, provides information about its activities.

CALIBNET

This network links 38 science and technology libraries in the Calcutta metropolitan area. The plan focuses on the introduction of automated systems into the participating libraries before networking them. Each library will have to automate its book acquisition, cataloguing, serials control, fund accounting and circulation control. Libraries participating in the CALIBNET will use AACR-2 for bibliographic description. The MAITRAYEE software, which supports MARC records, will enable records to be imported/exported through the CCF. CALIBNET will be linked to DELNET via dial-up access, and to external networks through the GPSS.

BONET

- Another landmark among the library networks of our country is BONET, which was inaugurated on 6 November, 1992 at the National Centre for Software Technology (NCST), Bombay. BONET is the latest project sponsored by NISSAT. The network has the following objectives:
  - to build a low cost library information system which can possibly be used as a model for future expansion of this service even outside Bombay;
  - to promote cooperation among libraries in Bombay with emphasis on interlibrary activities rather than computerizing individual libraries; and,

- To impart training related to library computerization and the networking of Bombay libraries.

This is just the beginning. In the years to come many libraries will be automated and linked to a network. This will result in reducing the expenditure incurred in purchasing journals, research materials, etc., and it will improve access to information

Natarajan (1990) discussed the progress in creating automated networks and role played by telecommunications in LAN. A LAN can readily replace much of the paper flow with electronic documents in an office environment.

SIRNET electronic mail system NISSAT New letter (1990) (Scientific and Industrial Research Network) developed for CSIR libraries located at INSDOC, New Delhi. It is concerned to larger network ERNET (Educational Research Network) and also acting as intravity mode for Delhi based CSIR laboratories and intercity node for other CSIR laboratories also act as a gateway to ERNET and through ERNET to international networks.

Meera, B.M. (1994) the author attempts is made to find out what LAN and WAN and the significance of WAN over LAN in the changing scenario of library resource sharing activities. The hardware and software requirements for the effective implementation of WAN are also studies.

Constraints of Networking

There are several constraints in the networking of Indian libraries. Higher education authorities still have a dilemma as to whether or not resource sharing is possible through networking. The potentialities of INFLIBNET are still not known to many academic libraries. Besides, UGC has failed to provide appropriate funds to academic libraries for computer software and hardware. Therefore, if INFLIBNET is to be of any help to the libraries, it surely has to provide funds for capital investment in software and hardware. These are the problems faced by the libraries:

- Information infrastructure is not up to date and there is a lack of trained manpower;

- Lack of effective networking and communication technology;
- Tardy implementation of proposed networks;
- Lack of uninterrupted power supply;
- Lack of foreign exchange for importing proper hardware;
- Technological backwardness, with a wide gap between India and developed countries.

Online Information System

Satyanarayana (1987) presented the development of online access to information system in a step by step fashion. The telecommunication alternatives productive interaction using aids, results of information retrieval practically bibliographic reference retrieval are covered.

Raina, Roshan Misra and Rajesh (1992) presents online information retrieval system frequently referred to as interactive or conversational system facilitate interaction between researchers and databases through computers and communication links. ORIS has emerged as a very powerful tool to bridge the gap between the ever increasing knowledge outputs on the one hand and ever increasing complex information needs of the users on the others in a most cost effective manner. Illustrating with practical example the paper discusses the merits or a good search strategy to arrive at a best precision level. Results can be cent-per cent target orient if the searcher commando analytical ability communication skills and assumes the role of a partner with the user in the search process.

Multimedia

Vijay Kumar K.P. (1997) attempts to survey the achievements already made and the landmark developments that are taking place in the telecommunication sector in India. It gives emphasis to the technology and the present state of affairs of the value-added service like radio paging, cellular telephones e-mail, data services, audio text, video text, video conference with where throw open to the private sector in this decade. It also covers the major telecommunications technologies that are considered for adoption in the country.

Rajasekhar T. B., Srinivas Ravi, A. and Neelameghan, A. (1998) OM Information Service (OMIS) provide web access to selected extracts from the writings and saying to spiritual leaders, saints, seers, mystics and scholars and also bibliographical sketches, and list of workers of some of these sources, web access has been made interesting through display of related images and rendering background music. The user and search interfaces have been designed for the novice user. OMIS is ported from a database originally available on CDS/ ISIS, the article discusses the content and structure of the CDS/ ISIS database requirements for the web and CD-ROM version, system design and implementation for the two media for the CD-ROM database access in currently provided by using windows version of CDS/ISIS operating as a helper application within the Netscape browser.

Multimedia is media and content that uses a combination of different content forms. The term can be used as a noun (a medium with multiple content forms) or as an adjective describing a medium as having multiple content forms. The term is used in contrast to media which only use traditional forms of printed or hand-produced material. Multimedia includes a combination of text, audio, images, animation, video and interactivity content forms.

Multimedia is usually recorded and played, displayed or accessed by information content processing devices, such as computerized and electronic devices, but can also be part of a live performance. *Multimedia* (as an adjective) also describes electronic media devices used to store and experience multimedia content. Multimedia is distinguished from mixed media in fine art; by including audio, for example, it has a broader scope. The term "rich media" is synonymous for interactive multimedia. Hypermedia can be considered one particular multimedia application.

Multimedia is simply multiple forms of media integrated

together. Media can be text, graphics, audio, animation, video, data, etc. An example of multimedia is a web page on the topic of Mozart that has text regarding the composer along with an audio file of some of his music and can even include a video of his music being played in a hall.

Besides multiple types of media being integrated with one another, multimedia can also stand for interactive types of media such as video games CD-ROMs that teach a foreign language, or an information Kiosk at a subway terminal. Other terms that are sometimes used for multimedia include hypermedia and rich media.

The term Multimedia is said to date back to 1965 and was used to describe a show by the Exploding Plastic Inevitable. The show included a performance that integrated music, cinema, special lighting and human performance. Today, the word multimedia is used quite frequently, from DVD's to CD-ROMs to even a magazine that includes text and pictures.

Multimedia Applications

Multimedia has become a huge force in American culture, industry and education. Practically any type of information we receive can be categorized as multimedia, from television, to magazines, to web pages, to movies, multimedia is a tremendous force in both informing the American public and entertaining us.

Advertising is perhaps one of the biggest industry's that use multimedia to send their message to the masses. Where one type of media, let's say radio or text can be a great way to promote an item, using multimedia techniques can significantly make an item being advertised better received by the masses and in many cases with greater results.

Multimedia in Education has been extremely effective in teaching individuals a wide range of subjects. The human brain learns using many senses such as sight and hearing. While a lecture can be extremely informative, a lecture that integrates pictures or video images can help an individual learn and retain information much more effectively. Using interactive CD

ROM's can be extremely effective in teaching students a wide variety of disciplines, most notably foreign language and music.

Multimedia and the Future

As technology progresses, so will multimedia. Today, there are plenty of new media technologies being used to create the complete multimedia experience. For instance, virtual reality integrates the sense of touch with video and audio media to immerse an individual into a virtual world. Other media technologies being developed include the sense of smell that can be transmitted via the Internet from one individual to another. Today's video games include bio feedback. In this instance, a shock or vibration is given to the game player when he or she crashes or gets killed in the game. In addition as computers increase their power new ways of integrating media will make the multimedia experience extremely intricate and exciting.

Multimedia is the encompass of all media used in electronics, particularly with computers. The use of computers to present text, graphics, video, animation and sound in an integrated way. Long touted as the future revolution in computing, multimedia applications were, until the mid-90s, uncommon due to the expensive hardware required. With increases in performance and decreases in price, however, multimedia is now commonplace. Nearly all Personal Computers are capable of displaying video, though the resolution available depends on the power of the computer's video adapter and microprocessor.

Interactive Multimedia is the means to interface with these media typically with a computer keyboard, mouse, touch screen, on screen buttons, and text entry allowing a user to make decisions as to what takes place next with this multimedia.

Digital Library

Definition : Digital Library is an information system targeted towards a specific community, where content from different sources is collected and managed, content is structured and enriched with metadata, and a set of services is offered that makes the content available to a user community via a communication network, typically the Internet.

Digital Libraries are the electronic counterparts of traditional paper libraries, where the digital medium opens new opportunities, especially in the area of improved access support, increased content availability, powerful content interlinking, and reduced costs, but also imposes new challenges like long-term preservation in the context of fast changing storage technologies. Further important challenges are issues of copyright and digital rights management and the cost of digitization for not digitally-born content.

Various definitions for Digital Libraries exist. These can be summarized as follows: A Digital Library is an information system targeted towards a specific community, where content from different sources is collected and managed, content is structured and enriched with metadata, and a set of services is offered that makes the content available to a user community via a communication network, typically the Internet.

Multimedia Libraries are Digital Libraries, where the managed content is not restricted to the usually mainly textual documents. Such libraries contain, next to the "textual" contents, media types like music, videos, images, maps, and mixtures of different content types (multimedia objects) as they are, for example used in e-Learning or in the documentation of history. Multimedia libraries may also contain content types that were not supported in traditional libraries at all like 3D objects, executable software (e.g. computer games) or callable services. One of the main challenges for a multimedia library is to provide effective access to these types of context (based on adequate indexing) and to provide support for the "real-time" integration of different content types. Some challenges of multimedia libraries are closely related to those of museums and archives that make multimedia representations of their artifacts available online.

The role of Digital Libraries in mediating between the individual information needs of the members of a community and the vast amount of globally available content. In this context the services provided by a library play a central role. Therefore, search services and further value adding services within a Digital Library are discussed next in the article with a focus on the special requirements of multimedia content. The article closes with some current trends and open research issues in Digital Library technology.

CD-ROM

Taneja (1991) describes CD-ROM items its applications recording and reading mechanisms, information retrieval methods and designing of retrieval software along with the system.

Components are discussed problems of standardization interchangeability are also touched. Role of CD-ROM in library resource sharing and networking has been examined. Bring out the points in favour as well as against CD-ROM and suggests the improvements needed to increase its utility selection methods and input of CD-ROM on libraries in India have been indicated.

Sonia Relan and Lakshmi Kakar (1993) described in details of CD-ROM systems databases and CD networking system available at DESIDOC. Advantages of Online and CD databases are compared. Problems faced in acquisition, installation of various databases and retrieval software problems of major CD database produces are also covered.

Jennifer Rowley (1995) discusses ways of evaluating GUI operations. Analyzes some of the computers of graphical user interfaces (GUI) applied to CD-ROM databases, (windows, dialogue boxes, menus, commands, buttons, check boxes and icons) and remarks on the degree to which these are based on window software. Notes the constraints to GUI's that sill remains even after databases have appeared in the market place; particularly mouse based problems. Discusses ways of evaluating GUI and their specific components and reports a study of database in which these types of interfaces are used, notes the significant variability between products in the way that they apply GUI's and discusses whether database use would benefit from a certain degree of the local user interface, concludes that the introduction of windows based CD-ROM databases with graphical user interfaces will increasingly revolutionize the design of such databases makes 3 recommendations that would aim to enhance the user. Evaluating interfaces in the GUI environments, standardization of interfaces design between some products, particularly for novice users; and facilities to allow experienced users to develop their own interface design.

Chakravarthi and Others (1995) discusses CD-ROM state of the art technology and industry technology and application trends analysis, new investments, new products/markets; new alliances inter and intra company's countries and market technology forecast as revealed in the literature are discussed.

Vijay Kumar and Others (1996) discussed in their article about the future plans of INFLIBNET. Networking of Indian Universities and R & D centers the way they are connected, the types of services it will offer and advantage there from are highlighted.

Lishan, Adam (1997) describes CD-ROM storage capacity, its integration with desktop a notebook computers and its combination with online networks make it an attractive technology for developing countries.

8

Data Analysis

This chapter presents analysis of the data gathered through the user survey and the findings. Analyzed data is displayed in the form of tables. Percentages are calculated to show the comparative analysis of the findings.

Objectives

- To ascertain information about the origin and development of the libraries surveyed.
- To gather details about the existing library facilities in terms of collections, staff, equipment and services.
- To collect information about the total budget and provisions made separately for computer facility if any.
- To review the present position of computer facility in the libraries surveyed in terms of space located, number of systems.
- To find out the activities, services and areas where computers are used in libraries.
- To know the problems faced by the librarians and libraries in automating their libraries partially or fully.
- To ascertain details about the future plans of the libraries in automating their libraries.
- To collect the opinions and suggestions of librarians for improving specific areas of computer applications in their libraries.

- To assess the information needs and information seeking behaviour of faculty.

Library Survey

Library Building

For providing effective library services, the college must have an attractive, spacious and well-equipped functional physical space and building for the library. The survey has attempted to find out the present status of the library building in the colleges surveyed. Details are shown in the following table.

Table – 8.1
Library Building

Sl. No.	*Opinion*	*Number*	*Percentage*
1.	Yes	4	40.00
2.	No	6	60.00
	Total	10	100.00

The above table shows the details about the location of the library building. It is evident from the table that out of ten colleges four colleges are having independent building for the library. Library is sharing the accommodation with other departments in the remaining colleges.

Table – 8.2
Total Area of Library Building in Sq. Mts

Sl. No.	*Area in Sq. Mts.*	*Number*	*Percentage*
1.	Up to - 2000	2	20.00
2.	2000 - 3000	4	40.00
3.	3000- 4000	2	20.00
4.	4000 and above	2	20.00
	Total	10	100.00

Table 8.2 shows the actual area of the library building in square meters. The physical space occupied by majority of the libraries (40%) is ranging between 2000 sq. mts. to 3000 sq. mts.

Two (20%) libraries are found to be occupying more than 4000 sq. mts. Only two (20%) libraries are operating in an area of less than 2000 sq. mts.

For effective execution of every activity in the library there is a need to provide separate accommodation for equipment and work area for staff. The following table indicates details about space provisions made for automation in the libraries surveyed.

Table – 8.3
Separate Accommodation for Automation Purposes

Sl. No.	*Opinion*	*Number*	*Percentage*
1.	Yes	6	60.00
2.	No	4	40.00
	Total	10	100.00

It may be observed from the analysis of data that out of 10 college libraries surveyed, majority (60%) are provided with separate accommodation for automation purposes.

Table – 8.4
Adequacy of Accommodation for Library Automation

Sl. No.	*Opinion*	*Number*	*Percentage*
1.	Yes	7	70.00
2.	No	3	30.00
	Total	10	100.00

Table 8.4 shows that in majority of the libraries (70%) existing accommodation is sufficient for library automation operations. There is a need to enhance in 30 per cent of the libraries executing the automated operations. The following table indicates about the plans of the librarian regarding the accommodation.

Table – 8.5
Future Plans to Expand the Library Accommodation

Sl. No.	*Opinion*	*Number*	*Percentage*
1.	Yes	6	60.00
2.	No	4	40.00
	Total	10	100.00

It may be noted from the above table that 60 per cent of the libraries are having plans to expand the accommodation in the library for automation purposes in the near future.

Library Budget

Budgetary provision for the library is the key factor in managing the library effectively and efficiently. Planned budget allocation is a prerequisite for scientific planning and utilization of financial resources. Following table indicate information regarding this aspect.

Table – 8.6
Planned Allocation of Budget

Sl. No.	*Opinion*	*Number*	*Percentage*
1.	Yes	7	70.00
2.	No	3	30.00
	Total	10	100.00

Table above shows the present status of the planned allocation of budget to the libraries surveyed. Majority of the libraries (70%) are receiving the budget allocation as per plan. Details regarding the budget allocation are presented in the next table.

Table – 8.7
Total Annual Budget

Sl. No.	*Range*	*Number*	*Percentage*
1.	Up to 3 Lacks	3	30.00
2.	3-4 Lacks	2	20.00
3.	4 Lacks and above	5	50.00
	Total	10	100.00

It may be observed from the above table that half of the libraries (50%) are being allocated an amount of more than 4 lakh of budget. Only 30 per cent of the libraries are receiving less than 3 lakh rupees of annual budget. However, in view of the increasing costs of books, journals and demands, the existing allocation may not be adequate. Next table shows the opinions of the librarians about the adequacy of funds.

Table – 8. 8
Opinion about Budget Allocation

Sl. No.	*Opinion*	*Number*	*Percentage*
1.	More than adequate	2	20.00
2.	Adequate	2	20.00
3.	Not adequate	6	60.00
	Total	10	100.00

Majority of the librarians (60%) felt that the budget allocation is not adequate for meeting the changing requirements of the users. Only 20 per cent stated that the budget is adequate.

Table – 8.9
Opinion on Budget Allocation for Automation

Sl. No.	*Description*	*Number*	*Percentage*
1.	More than adequate	2	20.00
2.	Adequate	2	20.00
3.	Not adequate	6	60.00
	Total	10	100.00

Table shows the opinion on budget allocation for automation. 60 per cent of the librarians felt that budget allocation for automation is not adequate. However, 20% of librarians felt that the allocation is adequate.

The study has also attempted to find out whether there is a separate allocation for computers maintenance in the budget.

Table – 8.10
Separate Allocation of Funds for Computers Maintenance

Sl. No.	*Description*	*Number*	*Percentage*
1.	Computer Maintenance	5	50.00
2.	Insurance	0	00.00
3.	Up-gradation	5	50.00
	Total	10	100.00

It may be noticed from the table above that, half of the libraries have separate annual allocation for maintenance of computers. Another half of the libraries are provided with separate fund for up-gradation of hardware of the computers.

Table – 8.11
Expenditure on Library Automation

Sl. No.	*Description*	*Number*	*Percentage*
1.	Below 50000	2	20.00
2.	50000-1000000	3	30.00
3.	3.1lack and above	5	50.00
	Total	10	100.00

Table 8.11 shows details of the amount spent by libraries on automation. Half of the libraries surveyed have spent more than three lakhs on library automation.

Software, Harware and Networking

Library automation implies the use of computers and other semi-automatic devices in various operations of the library. If further involves hardware and software selection and up-gradation, building of database, linking and networking with in library and with in the campus. Further library automation and networking enable the library to act as dynamic centre providing services online even to the remote users. The present survey describes in detail the efforts made by the libraries towards library automation and networking.

Local Area Network (LAN) is part of communication network limited to linking of computers with in the vicinity of 10 km distance. Usually LAN facility will be provided to connect the computer systems with in a single building or a small organization to access, retrieve, and share data from a centralized store called 'server'. The database management systems are being operated through LAN facility in organizations. Today a complete hardware and software solutions are available to the problem of sharing programme files, data files and peripherals and providing security for master files and personal information available through LAN. The present study has attempted to gather the details about the status of networking facility in the libraries surveyed.

Table –8.12
LAN (Local Area Network)

Sl. No.	*Opinion*	*Number*	*Percentage*
1.	Yes	6	60.00
2.	No	4	40.00
	Total	10	100.00

Table 8.12 indicates about the availability of LAN (Local Area Net work) facility. Out of ten libraries six libraries are having LAN facility within the building. The remaining four are not having Local Area Network (LAN) facility.

Table – 8.13
Library as Part of Campus Network

Sl. No.	*Opinion*	*Number*	*Percentage*
1.	Yes	2	20.00
2.	No	8	80.00
	Total	10	100.00

It may be noticed from the above table that only twenty per cent of the libraries surveyed are members of the campus network of the college.

Table – 8.14
Internet Connectivity in the Library

Sl. No.	*Opinion*	*Number*	*Percentage*
1.	Yes	6	60.00
2.	No	4	40.00
	Total	10	100.00

The analysis of the above table indicates that majority (60%) of the libraries surveyed have internet connectivity whereas 40 per cent does not have internet connectivity.

Table – 8.15
Type of Internet Connectivity

Sl. No.	*Type of Connectivity*	*Number*	*Percentage*
1.	Dial up	0	0.00
2.	Dedicated	0	0.00
3.	Broadband limited	2	33.33
4.	Broadband unlimited	4	66.67
5.	Any other	0	0.00
	Total	6	100.00

The results of the table indicate that out of 6 colleges which have Internet connectivity 4 (66.67%) have Broadband unlimited type of connectivity whereas 2 (33.33%) have broadband limited type of connectivity.

Now-a-days e-resources are also gaining importance as sources of information. Especially CD-ROM collections, online databases and e-journals are made available to users by all the prominent publishers

Table – 8.16
Separate Budget Allocation for E-resources

Sl. No.	*Opinion*	*Number*	*Percentage*
1.	Yes	2	20.00
2.	No	8	80.00
	Total	10	100.00

The responses from the librarians reveal that majority of the libraries (80%) do not have separate budget allocation for procuring and/or subscribing electronic resources.

Table – 8.17
Library as a Member of Consortia

Sl. No.	*Opinion*	*Number*	*Percentage*
1.	Yes	1	10.00
2.	No	9	90.00
	Total	10	100.00

It is clearly evident from the table above, except one library all the other libraries (90%) are not members of any consortia.

Collection

The value of library lies in its richness in terms of collections which satisfy the information requirements of users. The quality of library services also depends on the quality and adequacy of the collection developed. The present study assessed the strength of the libraries surveyed in terms of collection they hold. Table presents the details on collection.

Table – 8.18
Book Collection

Sl. No.	*Range*	*Number*	*Percentage*
1.	Less than 10000	2	20.00
2.	10000-25000	4	40.00
3.	25000-50000	1	10.00
4.	50000-100000	2	20.00
5.	100000-200000	1	10.00
	Total	10	100.00

It may be observed from the above table that majority of the libraries surveyed (40%) has library books ranging between 10000 to 25000. Only one library is found to be having book collection ranging between 1 lakh to 2 lakh volumes. Out of the ten libraries, only two libraries indicated that they hold less than 10,000 collections of books.

Table – 8.19
Printed Periodicals

Sl. No.	*Range*	*Indian*	*Foreign*	*total*
1.	1-50	7(70.00)	6(100.00)	13
2.	50-100	2(20.00)	0(00.00)	2
3.	100-150	1(10.00)	0(00.00)	1
	Total	10(100.00)	6(100.00)	16

Table 8.19 presents the printed periodicals subscribed by the libraries surveyed. Analysis of the table shows that majority of the libraries procure periodicals ranging between 1-50. However, it is found that one library is procuring between the range of 100-150.

Library Staff

Table – 8.20
Level of Training and Knowledge of the Professional Staff

Sl. No.	*Levels*	*Number*	*Percentage*
1.	Have basic knowledge	3	30.00
2.	Needs additional training	5	50.00
3.	Have advanced knowledge	2	20.00
4.	Any other	—	—
	Total	10	100.00

It is noticed from the above table that majority (50%) of the professional staff needs additional training to meet the ever changing needs of the user community. Only 20 per cent of the librarians have advanced knowledge.

Automation Status

Table – 8.21
Status of Automation of Your Library

Sl. No.	*Status*	*Number*	*Percentage*
1.	Fully automated	1	10.00
2.	Partially automated	5	50.00
3.	Planned, but not implemented	4	40.00
	total	10	100.00

Table 8.21 presents the automation status of the libraries surveyed. The analysis of the table shows that 50 per cent of the libraries are partially automated whereas 40 per cent have planned for automation but not implemented.

Cataloguing/Bibliographic Control

Table – 8.22
Availability of OPAC

Sl. No	*Opinion*	*Number*	*Percentage*
1.	Yes	7	70.00
2.	No	3	30.00
	Total	10	100.00

It may be noticed from the above table that majority (70%) of the libraries are providing OPAC (Online Public Access Catalogue) to their user community.

Table – 8.23
Library In-house Database

Sl. No.	*Opinion*	*Number*	*Percentage*
1.	Yes	5	50.00
2.	No	5	50.00
	Total	10	100.00

Table 8.23 shows that 5(50%) libraries are maintaining in-house database covering the library book collection while the remaining the 5 (50%) libraries have not developed any library database.

Table – 8.24
Format Used for Records

Sl. No.	*Description*	*Number*	*Percentage*
1.	MARC	3	30.00
2.	Partial MARC	3	30.00
3.	Non-MARC	4	40.00
	Total	10	100.00

Out of the 10 libraries surveyed, maximum number (40%) are using Non-MARC formats for their records. It is evident that only 30 per cent of the libraries are using the standard MARC formats.

Table – 8.25
System Accessibility to OPAC

Sl. No.	*Access*	*Number*	*Percentage*
1.	Independent systems	3	42.86
2.	LAN	2	28.57
3.	INTERNET	0	00.00
4.	Campus network	2	28.57
	Total	7	100.00

Table 8.25 presents the details about the system accessibility to OPAC (Online Public Access Catalogue). The results show that nearly 43 per cent libraries provide access to the OPAC with stand-alone systems, whereas 2 libraries (28.57) provide access through LAN and remaining two through campus network.

Table –8.26
Printing Facility for Patron

Sl. No.	*Opinion*	*Number*	*Percentage*
1.	Yes	5	50.00
2.	No	5	50.00
	Total	10	100.00

The above table indicates the availability of printer to the patrons. It is observed that 50 per cent of the libraries provided printer facility for their patrons.

Table – 8.27
Status of Card/Tradition Catalogue

Sl. No.	*Opinion*	*Number*	*Percentage*
1.	Discarded	1	10.00
2.	Only printed card Catalogue is available	3	30.00
3.	Only self list maintained	1	10.00
4.	Card catalogue also kept current	5	50.00
5.	Other	0	0.00
	Total	10	100.00

The status of card/traditional catalogue of the libraries surveyed shows that majority (50%) of the libraries still maintain old card facility for the users.

Table – 8.28
Opinion on OPAC

Sl. No.	*Opinion*	*Number*	*Percentage*
1.	Very much satisfied	2	20.00
2.	Satisfied	4	40.00
3.	Neutral	4	40.00
4.	Dissatisfied	0	0.00
5.	Very much dissatisfied	0	0.00
	Total	10	100.00

Table 8.28 indicates that opinion about OPAC facility provided by the libraries surveyed. The analysis shows that 40 per cent of the users are satisfied; whereas 20 per cent were very much satisfied with OPAC (Online Public Access Catalogue) facility.

Table – 8.29
Use of Readymade Catalogue Records from Other Libraries

Sl. No.	*Opinion*	*Number*	*Percentage*
1.	Yes	1	10.00
2.	No	9	90.00
	Total	10	100.00

It is noticed from the above table that majority of libraries (90%) have not utilizing the readymade catalogue records from other libraries.

Circulation

Table – 8.30
Automated Circulation of Material

Sl. No.	*Opinion*	*Number*	*Percentage*
1.	Yes	5	50.00
2.	No	2	20.00
3.	Have plans	3	30.00
	Total	10	100.00

Table 8.30 presents the details of the libraries, which are following automated circulation. The results indicate that 50 per cent of the libraries surveyed follow automated circulation system, while 30 per cent have plans for automated circulation.

Table – 8.31
Circulation System Integrated with OPAC

Sl. No.	*Opinion*	*Number*	*Percentage*
1.	Yes	6	60.00
2.	No	4	40.00
	Total	10	100.00

The results of the above table shows that 60 per cent of libraries surveyed have integrated their circulation system with OPAC (Online Public Access Catalogue).

Table – 8.32
Automated Circulation

Sl. No.	*Opinion*	*Number*	*Percentage*
1.	Yes	4	40.00
2.	No	6	60.00
	Total	10	100.00

It is observed from the above table that majority (60%) of libraries are not circulating their materials through their automated method.

Acquisition Collection Development

Table - 8.33
Automated Acquisition System

Sl. No.	*Opinion*	*Number*	*Percentage*
1.	Yes	4	40.00
2.	No	3	30.00
3.	Have plans	3	30.00
	Total	10	100.00

It is found from the above table that 40 per cent of libraries have implemented automated acquisition system, whereas 30 per cent have not gone for automated acquisition system while 30 per cent are planning for automated acquisition system.

Table – 8.34
Automated System Integrated with the OPAC

Sl. No.	*Opinion*	*Number*	*Percentage*
1.	Yes	4	40.00
2.	No	6	60.00
	Total	10	100.00

It is noticed from the above table that 60 per cent of libraries have not integrated their automated acquisition system with the OPAC.

Table – 8.35
Opinion on the Automated Acquisition System

Sl. No.	*Opinion*	*Number*	*Percentage*
1.	Very satisfied	0	0.00
2.	Satisfied	5	50.00
3.	Neutral	5	50.00
4.	Dissatisfied	0	0.00
5.	Very dissatisfied	0	0.00
	Total	10	100.00

The results of the above table indicate that 50 per cent of the librarians were satisfied with automated acquisition system whereas 50 per cent were neutral regarding their opinion.

Serials

Table – 8.36
Automated Serial Control

Sl. No.	*Opinion*	*Number*	*Percentage*
1.	Yes	2	20.00
2.	No	7	70.00
3.	Have plan	1	10.00
	Total	10	100.00

Table 8.36 shows that majority of the libraries 7(70%) have not developed automated Serial control. One library is having plans to implement automated Serial control system in the near future.

Table – 8.37
Serial System is an Integrated with OPAC

Sl. No.	*Opinion*	*Number*	*Percentage*
1.	Yes	2	20.00
2.	No	8	80.00
	Total	10	100.00

It is clearly evident from the results that 80 per cent of the libraries surveyed have not integrated their serial system with OPAC where as only 20 per cent have integrated their serial system with OPAC.

Other Areas of Automation

Table –8.38
Computerized Database for In-house Theses /Dissertations/Reports

Sl. No.	*Opinion*	*Number*	*Percentage*
1.	Yes	00	00.00
2.	No	10	100.00
	Total	10	100.00

The analysis of the above table reveals that none of the libraries surveyed have created computerized database for in house theses/dissertations/reports.

Commercial Databases

Table – 8.39
Provide Access to Online/CD-ROM Commercial Database

Sl. No.	*Opinion*	*Number*	*Percentage*
1.	Yes	2	20.00
2.	No	7	70.00
3.	Have plans to subscribe	1	10.00
	Total	10	100.0

It is observed from the above table that 70 per cent of libraries surveyed are not providing access to online/CD-ROM commercial databases, while 20 per cent of the libraries providing access. Remaining 10 per cent of the libraries have plans to subscribe to online/CD-ROM commercial databases.

CD-ROM Database

Table – 8.40
Have CD-ROM Database

Sl. No.	*Opinion*	*Number*	*Percentage*
1.	Yes	2	20.00
2.	No	4	40.00
3.	Have plan	4	40.00
	Total	10	100.00

The findings of the above table shows that 20 per cent of the libraries have CD-ROM databases, whereas 40 per cent of the libraries have plans to create CD-ROM databases. Out of the 10 libraries surveyed, 40 per cent of the libraries do not have CD-ROM databases.

Table – 8.41
Level of Demand for CD-ROM Database

Sl. No.	*Level*	*Number*	*Percentage*
1.	High	0	0.00
2.	Medium	2	100.00
3.	Low	0	0.00
	Total	2	100.00

Table 8.41 shows the level of demand for CD-ROM databases. It is found that the demand is medium in all the libraries surveyed.

Table – 8.42
Literature Search

Sl. No.	*Opinion*	*Number*	*Percentage*
1.	Library staff	5	50.00
2.	End-user	3	30.00
3.	Both	2	20.00
	Total	10	100.00

The data presented in the above table reveals that in half of the libraries library staff perform literature search, followed by end-users in the case of 30 per cent of the libraries.

Table – 8.43
Opinion on CD-ROM Database Services

Sl. No.	*Opinion*	*Number*	*Percentage*
1.	Very satisfied	0	0.00
2.	Satisfied	2	20.00
3.	Neutral	8	80.00
4.	Dissatisfied	0	0.00
5.	Very dissatisfied	0	0.00
	Total	10	100.00

The above table indicates opinion on CD-ROM database services. It was found that majority (80%) of libraries felt neutral, where as 20 per cent felt satisfied.

Table – 8.44
Use of Computers for Desktop Publishing

Sl. No.	*Opinion*	*Number*	*Percentage*
1.	Yes	0	0.00
2.	No	5	50.00
3.	Have plans	5	50.00
	Total	10	100.00

Table 8.44 indicates the user of computers for desktop publishing. The results clearly show that 50 per cent of the libraries have plan to user computers for desktop publishing whereas 50 per cent are not utilizing.

Table – 8.45
Other Computers Applications

Sl. No.	*Purposes*	*Number*	*Percentage*
1.	Office communications	6	60.00
2.	Report preparation	2	20.00
3.	Any other	2	20.00
	total	10	100.00

The above table presents the details about the general purpose for which the computers are used in the libraries. It is quite interesting to note that 60 per cent of the libraries surveyed use computers for office communications and only 20 per cent for report preparation.

Table – 8.46
Use of Computerized Spreadsheets

Sl. No.	*Opinion*	*Number*	*Percentage*
1.	Yes	2	20.00
2.	No	8	80.00
	Total	10	100.00

Table 8.46 shows data on the use of computerized spreadsheets. Out of the ten libraries 80 per cent of the libraries are not using computerized spreadsheets.

Table – 8.47
Users Training Programmes

Sl. No.	*Opinion*	*Number*	*Percentage*
1.	Yes	4	40.00
2.	No	6	60.00
	Total	10	100.00

It is evident from the above table that only 40 per cent of the libraries surveyed are providing training programmes to the library users whereas 60 per cent of the libraries are not providing any orientation to the freshman.

User Survey

Age Group

The sample taken for study consists of teachers of different age groups. In order to assess the prominent age groups in users, data has been gathered in this regard. The following table presents the details.

Table – 8.48
Age-wise Distribution of Faculty

Age	*No. of Teachers*	*(%)*
20 – 30	3	(13.64)
31 – 40	3	(13.64)
41 – 50	7	(31.82)
51 – 60	9	(41.91)
Total	22	(100.00%)

Analysis of data in the above table shows that majority of the teachers belongs to the age group 41 – 50 years (45.45%) followed by 51 – 60 years age group (41%). Only 13 per cent of the teachers in the sample are in the age group of 31 to 40 years.

Designation

Among the teachers, some have attained their promotions with their rich experience and research work. Table below shows the designation or cadres of teachers covered in the survey :

Table – 8.49
Designation

Age	*No. of Teachers*	*(%)*
Professor	—	
Associate Professor	6	(27.27)
Assistant Professor (Lecturers)	16	(72.73)
Others	—	
Total	22	(100.00)

From the table it is evident that majority of the teachers are Assistant Professors (72.73%). However, 27 per cent of them are Associate Professors.

Subject/Department

The libraries surveyed in the present study offers different degree courses in number of disciplines. Table indicates subject-wise categorization of the sample :

Table – 8.50
Subject/Department

Name of the Department	*No. of Teachers*	*(%)*
English	3	(13.64)
Zoology	4	(18.18)
Botany	4	(18.18)
Commerce	2	(9.09)
Chemistry	5	(22.73)
Physics	3	(13.64)
Hindi	1	(4.55)
Total	22	(100.00)

It may be observed from the table that highest per cent of the teachers responded to the survey are from Chemistry (23%), Botany (18%) and Zoology (18%).

Educational Qualifications

The present study has attempted to find out the educational qualifications of the faculty surveyed whose main activity is teaching the graduate students followed by research in their area of specialization. The following table presents the details about education qualifications of teachers.

Table – 8.51
Educational Qualifications

Qualification	*No. of Teachers*	*(%)*
Postgraduate	12	(54.54)
M.Phil	5	(22.73)
Ph.D	5	(22.73)
Any other	—	
Total	22	(100.00%)

It may be noticed from the above table that majority of the teachers (54%) are having only masters degree in their concerned field. Nearly 23 per cent of the faculty have doctorate and another 23 per cent of them are having M.Phil Degree.

Teaching Experience

Experience of teachers is also an important criterion that influences their extent of use of the library. Table below shows number of years of experience of teachers surveyed.

Table – 8.52
Teaching Experience

Years	*No. of Teachers*	*(%)*
1-10 years	3	(13.64)
11-15 years	2	(9.09)
16-20 years	5	(22.72)
21-25 years	8	(36.37)
26-30 years	4	(18.18)
Total	22	(100.00)

Majority of the teachers (36%) as shown in the table are having 21-25 year of experience followed by those having 16-20 years of experience (22%). Out of the total, 18 per cent are found to be having 26-30 years of experience in teaching.

Research Activity

Data on the teachers' involvement in research activity has been presented in the following table.

Table – 8.53
Research Activity

Engaged in Research	*No. of Faculty*	*(%)*
Yes	10	(45.46)
No	12	(54.54)
Total	22	(100.00)

It is evident from the above table that majority of the teacher are not involved in research activity. However, 45 per cent of the faculty have either got their doctorates or M.Phil's or yet to complete their research work.

Research Experience

In order to know the number of year of research experience the teachers were asked the details about their experience. The details are shown in the following table.

Table – 8.54
Research Experience

Years	*No. of Faculty*	*(%)*
0 – 5	6	(60.00)
6 – 10	4	(40.00)
11 – 15	—	—
16 – 20	—	—
Total	10	(100.00%)

It may be seen from the above table that majority of the teachers (60%) have 5 or below 5 years of research experience and the remaining 40 per cent are involved in research activity for a period ranging 6 to 10 years. None of the teachers surveyed have more than 10 years of research experience.

Research Projects

Involvement in various research projects by the teachers indicates the degree of productive research work undertaken by them. Details about projects financed by various agencies are shown in the table below.

Table – 8.55
Research Projects

	No. of Faculty			*Total*
	AICTE (sponsored)	*UGC (sponsored)*	*DST (sponsored)*	*(N=10)*
Research Projects	4 (40.00%)	4 (40.00%)	2 (20.00%)	10 (100.00%)

Analysis of data shows that 40 per cent of the projects are sponsored by AICTE. Another 40 per cent are doing research under UGC sanctions, whereas 20 per cent are working in DST sponsored projects.

Library Use

Extent of use of any library can be measured using the frequency of visits made by the users to the library. The next table indicates different frequencies with which the users are visiting the library.

Table – 8.56
Library Use

Frequency	*No. of Teachers*	*(%)*
(a) Every day	14	(63.64)
(b) Once in a week	5	(22.73)
(c) More than once a week	2	(9.09)
(d) Once in a fortnight	1	(4.55)
(e) Once in a month	—	
(f) Occasionally	—	
(g) Never	—	
Total	22	(100.00)

It can be observed from the table that majority of the teachers (63%) are regular visitors to the library. Every day they personally visit the library. Second highest per cent of users are found to be visiting the library once in a week (nearly 23%).

Time Spent in the Library

The present study also aims at ascertaining information about the time spent by the users in the library. Table-10 presents the details related to this aspect.

Table – 8.57
Time Spent in the Library

Hours	*No. of Faculty*	*(%)*
(a) More than 20 hours per week	—	
(b) 16 to 20 hours per week	5	(22.73)
(c) 11 to 15 hours per week	—	
(d) 7 to 10 hours per week	3	(13.63)
(e) 4 to 6 hours per week	12	(54.54)
(f) less than 4 hours per week	2	(9.09)
Total	22	(100.00)

Analysis of data reveals that majority of the teachers are spending 4 to 6 hours per week in the library (54.54%) followed by those teachers staying for 16 to 20 hours per week in the library (22.73%) for reference purposes.

Visits to Other Libraries

In order to know extent of dependency of the faculty on other libraries for required information, they are asked to give details about their visits to other libraries.

Table – 8.58
Use of Other Libraries

Use of other libraries	*No. of Faculty*	*(%)*
Yes	16	(72.73)
No	6	(27.27)
Total	22	(100.00)

It is evident from the analysis of data in the above table that majority of the teachers (72%) are depending on other libraries for required books and information.

Types of Libraries Visited

The following table presents the data on different types of libraries visited by the faculty.

Table – 8.59
Types of Libraries Visited

Types	*No. of Faculty*	*(%)*
Other college libraries	—	
University Library	11	(68.75)
Public Library	5	(31.25)
Library outside Hyderabad	—	
Total	16	(100.00)

Majority of the faculty (68%) are found to be visiting the University Library, whereas 31 per cent stated that they are referring the local public library.

Time Spent in Other Libraries

The extent of use of other libraries can be measured using number of hours the faculty prefers to spend in these libraries. Table shows the time duration spent by the teachers in other libraries.

Table – 8.60
Time Spent in Other Libraries

Time Spent	*No. of Faculty*	*(%)*
(a) Less than one hour	2	(12.50)
(b) One hour	5	(31.25)
(c) Two hours	4	(25.00)
(d) Three hours	4	(25.00)
(e) More than three hours	1	(6.25)
Total	16	(100.00)

From the analysis of data, it may be noticed that highest per cent of faculty (31%) are spending one hour in other libraries. Only 6 per cent of the faculties are spending more than three hours in other libraries.

Nature and Types of Information Required

The most important aspect of this study is to ascertain details on the nature of information required by the faculty. It also tries to find out the extent of dependency on each type of information preferred by the faculty. The users were asked to opt from among ten types of information listed in the questionnaire. The preferences of teachers are shown in the following table.

Table – 8.61
Type of Information Required

	Highly required	*Frequently required*	*Occasionally required*	*Total (N=22)*
(a) Review of literature (Annual reviews, year of books, state of art reports, recent advances, etc.)	12 (54.54%)	3 (13.64%)	6 (27.27%)	21 (95.45%)
(b) Theoretical background/ Basic scientific and technical information	11 (50.00%)	6 (27.27%)	4 (18.18%)	21 (95.45%)
(c) Methods, Process and Procedures	3 (13.64%)	9 (40.90%)	6 (27.27%)	18 (81.81%)
(d) Experimental designs, results and application	5 (22.72%)	8 (36.37%)	5 (22.72%)	18 (81.81%)
(e) Product, material, equipment and apparatus know-how information	3 (9.09%)	6 (27.27%)	9 (40.91%)	17 (77.27%)
(f) Information about previous work done if your field	6 (27.27%)	3 (13.64%)	4 (18.18%)	13 (59.09%)
(g) Information about current development in your field	7 (31.81%)	8 (36.37%)	2 (9.09%)	17 (77.27%)
(h) Management information	6 (27.27%)	4 (18.18%)	2 (9.09%)	12 (54.54%)
(i) Statistical Data	4 (18.18%)	4 (18.18%)	2 (9.09%)	10 (45.45%)
(j) Other type of information, if any, please specify	—	—	—	—

Among various options listed, majority of the faculty (95.45%) opted for the first two types of information viz., literature reviews and theoretical background/basics of scientific and technical information. The second highest per cent of the teachers (81%) preferred to use information on methods, process/products and experimental design, results and applications. Only 22 per cent of the faculty wanted statistical information.

The degree of dependency on different types of information shows that among various types highly required, literature reviews and books providing basic background to the subject are found to high. Among those items frequently referred items dealing with methods, processes and products are used by majority of the faculty. Regarding the types of information occasionally referred, highest per cent of faculty wanted product and know-how practical information (53%).

Motivating Factors Behind Seeking Information

There are number of reasons that motivate the teachers to use the library and information. Various options are listed out in the questionnaire to indicate the motivating forces by the faculty.

All the faculty members surveyed stated that for writing and publishing papers they visit the library and refer the library resources (100%). The second highest per cent of them (95.45%) required information for teaching purposes and for keeping themselves up-to-date in the latest knowledge and developments (95.45%). Other significant reasons that motivated the teachers include guiding the students, participation in seminars and for setting examination question papers.

Extent of Dependency on Different Types of Documents

The present study also aims at finding out the preferences of faculty for various document categories. Table 8.63 presents details on this aspect.

It is evident from the above table that all the teachers

Table – 8.62
Reasons for Seeking Information

	Non-motivator	*Weakest motivator*	*Average motivator*	*Fairly motivator*	*Strongest motivator*	*Total (N=22)*
(a) To prepare for class teaching	—	—	5 (22.73%)	4 (18.18%)	9 (40.90%)	18 (81.81%)
(b) To guide my students projects/ research scholars	—	—	7 (31.81%)	7 (31.81%)	8 (36.36%)	22 (100.00%)
(c) General awareness for new knowledge	—	—	11 (50.00%)	7 (31.81%)	4 (20.00%)	22 (100.00%)
(d) For participation in seminars/ conferences, etc.	—	1 (4.55%)	9 (40.90%)	—	8 (36.36%)	18 (81.81%)
(e) To write and publish papers	2 (9.09%)	—	7 (31.81%)	4 (18.18%)	8 (36.36%)	21 (95.45%)
(f) To setting up question papers, etc.	7 (31.81%)	—	3 (13.64%)	9 (40.90%)	2 (9.09%)	21 (95.45%)
(g) For pleasure of doing good work, self-fulfilment and self-satisfaction	1 (4.55)	—	7 (31.81%)	7 (31.81%)	7 (31.81%)	22 (100.00%)
(h) To have visibility among peers and colleagues	3 (13.64%)	3 (13.64%)	2 (9.09%)	2 (9.09%)	11 (50.00%)	18 (81.81%)
(i) Other reasons, if any, please specify	1 (4.55%)	2 (9.09%)	2 (9.09%)	—	4 (18.18%)	9 (40.90%)
(j) —	—	—	3 (13.64%)	1 (4.55%)	1 (4.55%)	5 (22.73%)

Table – 8.63
Extent of Depencency on Different Types of Document

	No depend-ness	*Rate depend-ness*	*Occasional depend-ness*	*Frequency depend-ness*	*High depend-ness*	*Total (N=2)*
(1)	(2)	(3)	(4)	(5)	(6)	(7)
(a) Books	—	—	3 (13.64%)	7 (31.82%)	10 (45.45%)	20 (90.91%)
(b) Handbooks/reference books	—	—	5 (22.73%)	9 (40.91%)	4 (18.18%)	18 (81.82%)
(c) Conference proceeding and papers	2 (9.09%)	2 (9.09%)	6 (27.27%)	2 (9.09%)	5 (22.73%)	17 (77.27%)
(d) Theses and dissertation	2 (9.09%)	3 (13.64%)	—	4 (18.18%)	9 (40.91%)	18 (81.82%)
(e) Current reading materials such as periodicals journals	3 (13.64%)	—	8 (36.36%)	3 (13.64%)	8 (36.36%)	22 (100.00%)
(f) Technical/R & D reports	3 (13.64%)	3 (13.64%)	2 (9.09%)	3 (13.64%)	7 (31.82%)	18 (81.82%)
(g) Standards and patent specifications	5 (22.73%)	—	4 (18.18%)	5 (22.73%)	1 (4.55%)	15 (68.18%)

Table – 8.63
Extent of Depencency on Different Types of Document

(1)	(2)	(3)	(4)	(5)	(6)	(7)
(h) Official documents including CSR/DST Publications	9 (40.91%)	—	—	5 (22.73%)	2 (9.09%)	16 (72.73%)
(i) Reprints and preprints from fellow professionals	6 (27.27%)	5 (22.73%)	2 (9.09%)	2 (9.09%)	4 (18.18%)	19 (86.36%)
(j) Abstracting and indexing journals including online CD ROM prints only	7 (31.82%)	—	—	—	3 (13.63%)	10 (45.45%)
(k) Trade catalogues from manufactures personal collections	6 (27.27%)	5 (22.73%)	—	—	1 (4.55%)	12 (54.55%)
(l) Audio/Video recordings	1 (4.55)	2 (9.09%)	7 (31.82%)	1 (4.55)	1 (4.55%)	12 (54.55%)
(m) Other formal sources, if any, please specify	—	3 (13.64%)	3 (13.64%)	3 (13.64%)	1 (4.55%)	10 (45.45%)

Table – 8.64
Extent of Depencency on Informal/Inter Personal Sources

	No depend-ness	*Rate depend-ness*	*Occasional depend-ness*	*Frequency depend-ness*	*High depend-ness*	*Total (N=2)*
(1)	(2)	(3)	(4)	(5)	(6)	(7)
(a) Personal experience	4 (18.18%)	3 (13.64%)	6 (27.27%)	7 (31.82%)	2 (9.09%)	22 (100.00%)
(b) Consulting experts in the field	—	3 (13.64%)	3 (13.64%)	3 (13.64%)	6 (27.27%)	15 (68.18%)
(c) Consulting colleagues and fellow professionals	—	4 (18.18%)	3 (13.64%)	—	6 (27.27%)	13 (59.09%)
(d) Results of one's own expenses	2 (9.09%)	5 (22.73%)	4 (18.18%)	—	3 (13.64%)	14 (63.64%)
(e) Consulting Library staff/ catalogues/OPAC's	3 (13.64%)	—	7 (31.82%)	4 (18.18%)	2 (9.09%)	16 (72.73%)
(f) Professional meetings, seminars, symposia and lecturer	—	—	8 (36.36%)	2 (9.09%)	6 (27.27%)	16 (72.73%)
(g) Educational and Training courses	—	3 (13.64%)	6 (27.27%)	—	6 (27.27%)	15 (68.18%)
(h) Fellow professional outside	—	2 (9.09%)	5 (22.73%)	—	6 (27.27%)	13 (59.09%)
(i) Order information sources, if any, please specify	3 (13.64%)	5 (22.73%)	2 (9.09%)	3 (13.64%)	3 (13.64%)	16 (72.73%)

surveyed are depending mostly on periodical articles (100%) followed by those depending on books (95.45%) and conference proceedings (95.45%). Nearly 73 per cent of the teachers are referring publications from government departments and research institutes followed by those using reprints and preprints from fellow professionals (64%).

Dependency on Information/Inter Personal Sources

To find out the extent of dependency of faculty on information sources, lists of options are given in the questionnaire. Table 8.64 presents the detailed analysis of data on this aspect.

All the teachers stated that they mostly depend on their knowledge gained through past experience. Nearly 73 per cent of the teachers also stated that they depend on library staff / catalogue/OPAC; professional meetings, seminars & conferences for required information. Nearly 68 per cent of the teachers also sought information from training programmes and workshops they have attended.

Use of Services

The faculty were also asked to rate the general and information services offered by the library. Table 8.65 shows the preferences for service.

Table – 8.65
Use of Services

	Margi-nally	*Substan-tially*	*Comple-tely*	*Total* (N = 22)
1	2	3	4	5
(a) Loan of books	4 (26.66%)	8 (53.33%)	3 (20.00%)	15 (68.18%)
(b) Reference services	4 (30.76%)	6 (46.15%)	3 (23.07%)	13 (59.09%)
(c) Bibliographical Services	4 (28.57%)	7 (50.00%)	3 (21.43%)	14 (63.64%)
(d) Current Awareness Service (e.g. List of additions)	5 (31.25%)	3 (18.75%)	8 (50.00%)	16 (72.72%)

1	2	3	4	5
(e) Inter library loan	3 (17.64%)	9 (58.82%)	5 (29.41%)	17 (77.27%)
(f) Reprographic Services	5 (50.00%)	4 (40.00%)	1 (10.00%)	10 (45.45%)
(g) CD-ROM Printouts	9 (64.28%)	3 (21.43%)	2 (14.28%)	14 (63.64%)
(h) Journals/periodicals Circulations	6 (37.50%)	6 (31.25%)	6 (31.25%)	16 (72.72%)
(i) Other services, if any, specify	1 (10.00%)	2 (20.00%)	2 (12.00%)	5 (22.72%)

Among various services listed, majority of the faculty (77%) are found to be using reprographic service offered by the library. The second highest per cent (72%) are found to be using current awareness services and periodical collections. Nearly 68 per cent are using the library loan facility.

Methods/Approaches of Getting Required Information

There are different ways users follow to get required information or book from the library. Different sources that help in locating the available information are listed in the questionnaire.

Table – 8.66
Approaches Followed to Get Required Items

Source Approached	*No. of Faculty*	*(%)*
1	2	*3*
(a) Library catalogue	14	(63.64)
(b) Abstracting and indexing periodicals journals	7	(31.82)
(c) Reference from bibliographies and review literature	9	(40.90)
(d) Latest additions list of library	12	(54.55)
(e) Citations (References) in current reading materials such as books, reports and periodicals/journals articles	7	(31.82)
(f) Announcements from publishers/ book-sellers	8	(36.36)

1	2	3
(g) Browsing in library shelves	8	(36.36)
(h) Browsing in books shops	9	(40.90)
(i) Browsing in INTERNET	10	(45.45)
(j) Consulting specialists in the field	9	(40.90)
(k) Consulting colleagues and fellow professionals	8	(36.36)
(l) Consulting library staff	8	(36.36)
(m) Other reasons, if any, please specify	—	

Analysis of data in the above table indicates that majority of the faculty approached the library catalogue (64%) to know about the required item. The second highest per cent of them (55%) referred the list of latest additions to the library for finding the required title. Nearly 45 per cent browsed the Internet to know about the latest publications in their field of interest. Bibliographies and Reviews also helped 40 per cent of the users to know about required books.

Reasons for not Using the Library Frequently

Some of the faculty members are not the regular users of the library. In order to find out the reasons for not using the library, a question with different options was posed to the respondents. Table 8.67 shows their responses.

Table – 8.67
Reasons for not Using/Visiting the Library

Reasons	*No. of Faculty*	*(%)*
1	2	3
(a) Lack of time	7	(31.82)
(b) Inconvenient location	5	(22.73)
(c) Location unsafe at night	—	
(d) Can't find what I needed	5	(22.73)
(e) Library staff are unfriendly	—	
(f) Library staff provide inefficient service	—	

Table – 8.68
Dependency on Services for Teaching and Research

	Teaching				*Total*	*Research*				*Total*
	Low	*Occasional*	*Frequent*	*High*		*Low*	*Occasional*	*Frequent*	*High*	
(a) Books			11 (50.00%)	5 (22.73%)	16 (72%)	—	—	2 (9.09%)	6 (27.27%)	8 (36%)
(b) Articles in Journals	2 (9.09%)	6 (27.27%)	2 (9.09%)	3 (13.64%)	13 (59%)	7 (31.81%)	2 (9.09%)	—	2 (9.09%)	11 (50%)
(c) News papers	2 (9.09%)	2 (9.09%)	3 (13.64%)	2 (9.09%)	9 (41%)	—	—	—	2 (9.09%)	2 (9%)
(d) Internet Services				2 (9.09%)	2 (9.09%)		2 (9.09%)	—	6 (27.27%)	8 (36%)
(e) Other, if any			2 (9.09%)	2 (9.09%)	4 (18%)	—	—	—	—	—

Table – 8.69
Level of Satisfasction

	Teaching				Total	Research				Total
	Satisfied	*Moderately Satisfied*	*Less Satisfied*	*Not Satisfied*		*Satisfied*	*Moderately Satisfied*	*Less Satisfied*	*Not Satisfied*	
(a) Books	5 (22.73%)	8 (36.36%)	—	4 (18.18%)		6 (27.27%)	2 (9.09%)	4 (18.18%)	—	
(b) Articles in Journals	2 (9.09%)	17 (77.27%)	2 (9.09%)	—		4 (18.18%)	5 (22.73%)	—	—	
(c) News papers	8 (40.00%)	10 (50.00%)	2 (10.00%)	—		4 (22.73%)	—	—	—	
(d) Internet Services	4 (22.73%)		2 (9.09%)	2 (9.09%)		4 (22.73%)	—	—	4 (22.73%)	
(e) Other, if any	4 (22.73%)		2 (9.09%)			4 (22.73%)	—	—	—	

1	2	3
(g) Don't have a library card	7	(31.82)
(h) Don't have communication facilities like E-Mail, Fax, etc.	4	(18.18%)
(i) Required materials are not in the library	3	(13.64%)
(j) Other reasons, if any, please specify	——	

All the teachers have not responded to this question. Among those answered, majority stated that due to lack of time they could not use the library (32%). Nearly 23 per cent also stated that they have not visited library, the library collection do not contain the material required by them.

Dependency on Library Resources for Teaching and Research

The present surveys have also gathered details regarding the level of dependency of teachers on library resources for teaching and research work. Table 8.68 presents the details.

The analysis of data shows that majority of the teachers (72%) are depending on books for teaching purposes followed by journal articles. But, few of them are found to be using Internet for teaching purpose.

Majority of the faculty found to be depending on periodicals (50%) first and Internet in the second place (36%) for research purpose. Significant per cent (36%) of them are also depending on latest books for the save of research.

Level of Satisfaction

The users were also asked to indicate their level of satisfaction regarding the sources available for teaching and research. Table 8.69 presents the details.

Majority of the faculty are found to be moderately satisfied with the collections. Most of them are not satisfied with the journal collections and the Internet services. The same types of responses are noticed even in the case of using the library resources for research purpose.

9

Conclusions and Suggestions

The conclusions drawn from the Library Survey and User Survey have been presented under sections 5.1 and 5.2 respectively in the following paragraphs. This chapter also presents the suggestions offered by the researcher for further improvement of library performance and services using IT in different areas of library applications under section 5.3.

Conclusions from Library Survey

Library Building

As far as library building is concerned, it is evident that out of ten colleges four colleges are having independent building whereas in other six colleges library is sharing accommodation with other departments. The physical space occupied by majority of the libraries (40%) is ranging between 2000 sq. mts. to 3000 sq. mts. Two (20%) libraries are found to be occupying more than 4000 sq. mts. Only two (20%) libraries are operating in an area of less than 2000 sq. mts. Majority of the libraries have provided separate accommodation for automation purpose. The study also revealed that the existing accommodation is sufficient for automation purposes in the majority of the libraries surveyed.

Library Budget

The examination of budget allocation in the libraries surveyed in the present study indicates that 70 per cent of the libraries have provision for budget and 30 per cent of the libraries do not have any allocation of budget. The total annual budget was 4 lakhs and above in 50 per cent of the libraries, whereas it was less than 3 lakhs in 30 per cent of the libraries. Majority of the librarians are of the opinion that budget allocation is not adequate to meet the requirements whereas 20 per cent found the budget allocation as adequate, while the other 20 per cent found it to be inadequate. As far as budget allocation for automation purposes is concerned, most of the librarians felt unhappy with the amount allocated for automation of the library. 50 per cent of the libraries have separate allocation in budget for computers maintenance and other 50 per cent of the libraries have separate budget for up-gradation of hardware. The expenditure on library automation in majority of the libraries was found to be 3 lakhs and above.

Software, Hardware and Networking

The survey of LAN (Local Area Network) facility in the libraries have revealed that out of ten libraries, six libraries are having LAN facility within the library building and the remaining four are not having LAN (Local Area Network) facility. Only two libraries are found to be part of their campus network. Regarding Internet connectivity is concerned, majority of the libraries surveyed (60%) are providing internet connectivity whereas 40 per cent does not have connectivity. The type of Internet connectivity reveals that majority of the libraries (66.67%) go for broadband unlimited while 33.33 per cent go for broadband limited. Majority of the libraries (80%) does not have separate budget allocation for E-Resources, while 20 per cent of the libraries surveyed do not provide allocation for E-Resources. Regarding consortia membership is concerned; most of the libraries (90%) are not member of any consortia while 10 per cent libraries are member of consortia.

Collection

The examination of the collection in the libraries surveyed, clearly depicted that majority of the libraries (40%) have collection ranging between 10000 to 25000, while 20 per cent of the libraries have collection ranging between 50000 to100000. It is interesting to note that out of ten libraries only one library has collection more than 1000000. As far as printed periodicals are concerned most of the libraries subscribe between the ranges of 1-50.

Library Staff

The level of knowledge and training of the professional staff working in the libraries surveyed clearly depicted that 50 per cent of the librarians require additional training; whereas 30 per cent of the librarians have basic knowledge, while 20 per cent of the professional staff have advanced knowledge in computer applications.

Automation Status and Cataloguing/Bibliographic Control

The results of the study indicate that 50 per cent of the libraries surveyed are partially automated, 40 per cent have planned for automation but not yet implemented and only a meager 10 per cent are fully automated. Majority of the libraries provide access to OPAC (Online Public Access Catalogue) through other model, whereas 20 per cent provide access to OPAC through Remote access. Out of ten libraries, 50 per cent of the libraries are providing printer to the patron, while the rest 50 per cent does not provide printer to the patrons of the library. The status of card/traditional catalogue reveals that 50 per cent of the libraries are still utilizing the old card facility, while only one library have discarded the traditional catalogue. Regarding the opinion about OPAC, it was found that 40 per cent of the users are satisfied; whereas 20 per cent were very satisfied with OPAC (Online Public Access Catalogue) facility.

Majority of the libraries (90%) in the present study does not use readymade catalogues from other libraries, while only one library (10%) is utilizing the readymade catalogue records from other libraries. The results of the study shows that 5(50%) libraries are maintaining in-house database covering the library book collection while the remaining the 5 (50%) libraries have not developed any library database.

Circulation

The examination of circulation aspect of the libraries surveyed in the present study depicts that 50 per cent of the libraries have implemented automated circulation system where as 30 per cent of the libraries have plan to implement automated circulation. Majority of the libraries have integrated their circulation with the OPAC (Online Public Access Catalogue) system. It is found that 60 per cent of the libraries were not issuing library material through automated circulation system.

Acquisition and Collection Development

The results of the study clearly indicate that 40 per cent of the libraries surveyed have implemented automated acquisition system whereas 30 per cent have plans to implement the system and 30 per cent of the libraries does not follow automated acquisition system. A study to reveal whether the libraries have integrated their automated acquisition system with OPAC revealed that 60 per cent have integrated their acquisition system with OPAC whereas 40 per cent have not integrated with OPAC. Majority of the libraries does not procure their library material through the automated acquisition system. The results indicate that 50 per cent of the librarians were satisfied with automated acquisition system whereas 50 per cent were neutral regarding their opinion.

Serials

A study to identify whether serials are issued through automated circulation system have revealed that 70 per cent of the libraries were not implementing the system, whereas 20 per cent of the libraries were following the system and 10 per cent of the libraries have plans to implement the system. It is observed from the results that majority of the libraries (80%) have not integrated their serial system with OPAC (Online Public Access Catalogue).

Other Areas of Automation

The results of the present study clearly indicate that no library surveyed have created a database for in house thesis/ dissertations/reports. Majority of the libraries (70%) do not provide access to online/CD-ROM commercial databases. As far as, availability of CD-ROM databases is concerned, the results are evenly scattered. 40 per cent of the libraries have plans to create CD-ROM databases, and 20 per cent of the libraries surveyed have already providing CD-ROM databases to the users. The level of demand for CD-ROM databases was found to be medium in all the libraries surveyed in the present study. A study to identify whether who performs the maximum number of searches, depicted that library staff with 50 per cent stood in the first place, followed by end-users with 30 per cent. Majority of the librarians were neutral on their opinion about CD-ROM database services, while 20 per cent were satisfied. 50 per cent of the libraries are using computers for desktop publishing while 50 per cent were not utilizing computers for desktop publishing. Majority of the libraries surveyed in the present study utilize computers for office communications (60%), followed by report preparations (20%). 80 per cent of the libraries were not utilizing the computerized worksheets in their daily work, whereas 20 per cent of the libraries are using them for their work. It is clear that out of ten libraries surveyed, only four (40%) are offering user orientation programmes so that they can utilize the services of the library in more efficient and effective manner.

Conclusions from User Survey

Age Group

The examination of the results indicate that majority of the teachers belongs to the age group 41 – 50 years (45.45%) followed by 51 – 60 years age group (41%).

Designation

The results of the study clearly depict majority of the teachers are Assistant Professors (72.73%). However 27.27 per cent are Associate Professors. It is quite interesting that there are no professors in the libraries surveyed.

Subject/Department

It is observed from the results that highest per cent of the teachers responded to the survey are from Chemistry (23%) followed by Botany (18%) and Zoology (18%).

Educational Qualifications

Out of the 22 respondents to the survey, only a small per cent of the teachers have procured their Doctoral Degrees i.e., Ph.D.'s (22.73%), M.Phil (22.73%) and Postgraduates (54.54%).

Teaching Experience

Majority of the teachers (36%) are having 25 year of experience followed by those having 20 years of experience (22%). Out of the total, 18 per cent are found to be having 30 years experience in teaching. The overall data shows that more than 77 per cent of the teachers are well experienced with minimum of 20 years service. However, 22 per cent of the teachers are found to be having experience below 15 years.

Research Activity

The study to identify the research activity among the teachers surveyed, have clearly indicated that majority of the teachers (54.45%) are not involved in the research activities.

Research Experience

It is evident from the results that majority of the teachers (60%) have 5 or below 5 years of research experience and the remaining 40 per cent are involved in research activity for a period ranging 6 to 10 years. None of the teachers surveyed have more than 10 years of research experience.

Research Projects

It is evident from the results that 40 per cent of the projects are sponsored by AICTE. Another 40 per cent are doing research under UGC sanctions whereas 20 per cent are working in DST sponsored projects.

Library Use

The results indicate that majority (63.64%) of the teachers surveyed in the present study are regular visitors to the library, followed by teachers who visit the library once in a week.

Time Spent in the Library

It is clear from the analysis, that majority (54.54%) of the teachers spends 4-6 hours per week in the library, followed by teachers (22.73% staying 16-20 hours per week in the library.

Visits to Other Libraries

Majority of the teachers surveyed in the present study have stated that they depend upon other libraries for their information requirements.

Type of Libraries Visited

Majority of the faculty (68%) are found to be visiting the University Library whereas 31 per cent stated that they are referring the local public library.

Time Spent in Other Libraries

The examination of the results clearly indicates that highest per cent of faculty (31%) are spending one hour in other libraries. Only 6 per cent of the faculty is spending more than three hours in other libraries.

Type of Information Required

The results depict that the majority faculty (95.45%) require literature reviews and theoretical background/basics of scientific and technical information. The second highest per cent of the teachers (81%) preferred to use information on methods, process/products and experimental design, results and applications. Only 22 per cent of the faculty wanted statistical information.

Motivating Factors Behind Seeking Information

All the faculty members surveyed stated that for writing and publishing papers they visit the library and refer the library resources (100%). The second highest per cent of them (95.45%) required information for teaching purposes and for keeping themselves up-to-date in the latest knowledge and developments (95.45%). Other significant reasons that motivated the teachers include guiding the students, participation in seminars and for setting examination question papers.

Extent of Dependency of Different Types of Documents

The study to identify the dependence of faculty surveyed on different forms of documents revealed that all the teachers surveyed are depending mostly on periodical articles (100%) followed by those depending on books (95.45%) and conference proceedings (95.45%).

Dependency on Information/Inter Personal Sources

The results indicate that the teachers surveyed in the present study mainly depend on the knowledge gained through their personal experience, followed by library staff/catalogue/OPAC.

Use of Services

In order to identify the services mostly used by the teachers surveyed, it was found that majority of them (77%) use the Inter-library Loan, followed by Current awareness services with 72 per cent.

Methods or Approaches of Getting Required Information

Analysis of data indicates that majority of the faculty approached the library catalogue (64%) to know about the required item. The second highest per cent of them (55%) referred the list of latest additions to the library for finding the required title.

Reasons for not Using Library Frequently

Lack of time; non-availability of the required material; lack of communication facilities like E-Mail, Fax; inconvenient location of the library were cited as reasons for not visiting the library frequently by the teachers surveyed in the present study.

Dependence on Library Resources for Teaching and Research

The teachers surveyed in the present study have revealed that they depend upon books followed by journals and internet for teaching purpose, whereas for research they mainly depend on periodical articles followed by Internet.

Level of Satisfaction

Majority of the faculty are found to be moderately satisfied with the collections. Most of them are not satisfied with the journal collections and the Internet services.

Suggestions

This study has identified the importance of I.T. in satisfying information seeking behavior of users in the degree colleges. The information needs and information seeking behaviour of users differ from person to person. On analyzing the data a number of findings and observations have been noticed in this study. The findings and observations necessitated the formulation of suggestions to enhance the capabilities of information seeking behaviour and to optimize the information resources of the medical college libraries. In this study it has been found that a few services such as book lending, periodical, reference and internet are only high ranked services found from the library. The pursuit of knowledge has been revolutionized, mainly through the vast expansion of information accessible via the networked systems. Increased knowledge of the information-seeking behaviours of users is crucial to meet their information needs. We can understand how electronic information resources strengthen the information-seeking processes. It is obvious how technology contributes to and perhaps alters the information-seeking process, and explores the applicability of digital information environment. So information Services and systems should be improved to better services to users as they navigate this new data-rich environment keeping in view of the importance of variety of documentation and ICT enabled services. It is suggested that all Government and non-government degree colleges should provide such services. To promote the awareness of such services the librarians should conduct user education programmes for promotion of the availability of library services and resources. It also possible to find out the extent of non-utilization of library services.

Technology, networking and media of information sources and services represent a combination of factors, which affect librarians. Technological advances suggest that the nature of library operations and possibly the social role of library may change. Technologies which can be used to collect, acquire, process, store, transmit and disseminate information are usually known as information technologies.

Technology is a comprehensive term, which includes a number of technologies like computers, telecommunications and optical digital systems. Information technologies have greatly influenced all the sectors like education, research, commerce, industry, health care, public administration and libraries are no exception.

- The information technologies that are relevant to libraries and information centres are computer technologies, telecommunication technologies, reprographic technologies, library technologies, technical communication. The details of the activities covered by these technologies are as follows :
  - *Computer technologies* — Database organization and Management and Library management operations.
  - *Telecommunication technologies* — Library networks, Information networks.
  - *Reprographic technologies* — Photography, Microfilms, Optical/Digital, Audio/Video.
  - *Library Technologies* — Classification, Cataloguing/ Indexing, Database creation, CAS, SDI.

Development of Information Technology in India

The development of information technology has great impact on all the sectors. It is quite interesting that even in a developing country like India, computers are used in schools, colleges, commercial shops, small trading units etc. apart from advanced educational and research institutions. A number of information networks are in operation like Education and Research Network (ERNET) of the Department of Electronics for communicating education and research information, National Informatics Centre Network (NICNET) of the Planning Commission for providing access as well as communicating governmental data and information; I-Net, a public data network provided by the Department of Telecommunications; and Videsh Sanchar Nigam Limited (VSNL) information network, for providing e-mail and Internet services. Many Libraries and Information centres in our country are utilizing the reprographic technologies of CD-ROMs, optical digital discs and multimedia systems. Several agencies in the government and in the trade are producing multimedia products and CD-ROM and online databases. Although, the number of such indigenous online databases and CD-ROM products is presently not high, it is expected to grow exponentially soon after the high capacity information networks and information highways become available. A national IT task force was constituted in May 1998 in order to give a boost to the use of IT in various sectors in the country. A major recommendation made by committee was to develop information content in the form of databases and other information products. In this context, there is a great opportunity for the library professionals to play a crucial role in the National IT plan.

Information Technology and Libraries

Information technology has a great impact on the activities of the libraries. Generally, main activities in any library include:

- Collection development (acquisition).
- Cataloguing and Classification.
- Circulation.
- Reference work.
- Preservation, Conservation and archiving.

With the application of Information technology gadgets, the activities of the libraries have undergone drastic change.

- **Collection Development:** Rising costs of printed publications, shrinking library budgets and information explosion have forced the librarians to shift their focus to literature or information available in databases and online systems. Procurement through Internet has also become common.
- **Cataloguing and Classification:** With the development of Information technology, a new revolution named OPAC (Online Public Access Catalogue) has replaced

the traditional catalogue in the libraries. OPAC enables the users to browse the holdings of the library without much difficulty, which saves the time of the users and in turn satisfies the S.R. Ranganthan Law "Save the time of the reader". As far as classification is concerned, Library of Congress, OCLC are providing the classification number which saves the time of the Library staff in classifying the documents.

- **Circulation:** Many of the libraries have gone for automated circulation system. This enables effective and efficient services to the user community and saving of time to the library staff. As most of the journals and books are procured, online (for example AICTE-INDEST Consortium, J-Gate, EBSCO, Ebrary.com) borrowing of library collections is reduced to some extent.
- **Reference Work:** The reference librarian can utilize the fruits of information technology gadgets like OPAC (Online Public Access Catalogue), Internet and other networks for providing reference service to the user community in minimum time possible.
- **Preservation and Archiving:** As the modern day libraries are mostly going for electronic forms like CD-ROM and multimedia, the preservation measures cover these media also.

IT and its Impact on the Development of Libraries

The library professionals can observe the impact of the IT on the future functioning of the libraries. The libraries in the future will have collections in multiple media, their activities and services fully automated, be networked, use internet and other information networks. However the extent of use of these facilities will vary from library to library. The observations of some of the experts who have made detailed studies about future libraries are worth noting.

The experts have visualized the future libraries in the following categories :

- **Polymedia Libraries:** The collection in this type of libraries includes independent media like paper, microfilm, compact disc etc. The organizational and management processes within these libraries are basically manual in nature.
- **Electronic Libraries:** The main feature of this library are extensive use of computers and other facilities like online databases and automated record keeping and computer-based decision making.
- **Digital Libraries:** In which information exists only in digital electronic format. The users can access the information available in digital form simultaneously at fast pace and low cost. The traditional library can hold only one or two copies of a book to its users, whereas the digital library can generate unlimited number of copies.
- **Virtual Libraries:** This type of libraries uses the technology of Virtual Reality (VR). In this environment, the user would be able to browse around a library system without having physically go to it. This form of libraries enables the users to enter the library, browse around its rooms and shelves, use an index or catalogue, select a book, open it and read it. Of course, the only place where the book really exists is in the computer and within the minds of the readers.

Application of IT in Indian Libraries

Although several attempts have been made since 1970's, the use of IT in libraries has been slow. In the initial phase some libraries attached to IIT Madras, CSIR have started automating some of their activities and services.

In the present situation, number of libraries in the country have gone for library automation, have e-mail and Internet facilities and acquire CD-ROM and multimedia publications. Several software like CDS/ISIS, WINISIS, SOUL, LIBSYS, LIBRIS, and SANJAY etc. have been developed and are in use in many libraries. A good number of city-based library networks are in operation like DELNET (Delhi Library Network), CALIBNET (Calcutta Library Network), MALIBNET (Madras Library Network), BONET (Bombay Library Network), and national level library network INFLIBNET (Information and Library Network) to cover all the University libraries in the country and it is sponsored by UGC. Majority of the libraries are including CD-ROM databases, composite publications in their collection.

Librarians and their Role in Future Libraries

The advanced countries have already recognized the importance of information content development, which is evident from the thousands of databases, developed and made available by these countries in various forms as online databases, CD-ROM/Multimedia databases. Similarly, the role of libraries in national development is also recognized in various countries. Now-a-days Library and Information Science sector has been identified as an important sector for an economy.

Data organization, structuring and presentation skills are essential for information content development, so that the users can access information easily. These skills are incorporated in the curriculum of Library and Information Science.

The library and information science professionals are best suited for the content development work and they have to grab the opportunity with both hands in order to get global recognition for the profession. The departments of the Universities have to restructure their curriculum, which enables the professionals to handle the challenge posed by Information technology revolution. The future librarian's have to more and more involved in information analysis and repackaging rather than providing documents. Therefore, the role of librarians will be knowledge managers and information analysts in the future.

- In order to survive and compete in the world of electronic information, today's information professionals have to develop new skills and strategies.

To be able to survive in the digital and the end-user-oriented era, re-engineering might be the only solution. A few critical elements of re-engineering of library activities by the library professionals include:

- The role of library and information professional changes from one of producing data and information to one of integrating new information technologies in providing effective information services.
- They will perform the creative tasks of information product development and product synthesis – thus providing information solutions and not just information.

Application of IT in Libraries: Issues and Challenges

- Many technological experts are of the opinion that IT can provide solution to all the information problems. They predict that future libraries will have no printed documents and no walls and they will be digital, cyber and virtual libraries, and disseminate information through networks. However, the library professionals are aware that the paper editions will not disappear from the library and they will increase along with digital editions of publications. Some of the problems related to digital collections are discussed below:
- Comfortable reading is possible with printed publications when one has to read continuously. The libraries of the future, which are designed to accommodate more digital collections, face a problem for providing space for print-based collections.
- As we can observe rapid changes in IT, the CD-ROM technology is likely to be replaced by DVDs. So the libraries which spent huge amounts on CD-ROM collections will have to again invest huge investments for procuring the new technology i.e. DVDs.
- Even though Internet is considered as most important source of information, it is often compared to a large

library without a catalogue leading to chaos. In this context, the academicians and researchers mostly prefer paper based scholarly publications to internet editions. The information provided in Internet is not authentic and accurate.

- The report of a survey conducted revealed that librarians generally take less time to provide information from library collection than from Internet. A paper published in 'Communications of the ACM (1995)' also advises, *"If you are in a hurry, go to the library, not to the Internet"*. The statement indicates the importance of the library even in this IT revolutionized era.
- A large number of catalogues are available on the Internet. However, even after searching the book it is difficult to procure the book. The traditional ILL (Inter-Library Loan) will help the document supply.
- The conversion of existing library collections into digital libraries is a difficult task keeping in view the associated software, human skills and copyright problems.
- Despite of all the shortcomings, it is known fact that digital or electronic collections will grow year by year. However, it is clear that along with digital and electronic collections the traditional paper-based publications are also going to increase in the libraries. Therefore, the present day librarians should be in position to handle both the current and traditional forms of collections.

As quoted by Dr. S.S. Murthy, the role of librarians will be:

- to utilize the current information technologies for providing effective and efficient services to the user community.
- to develop as an integrator of information and as an information intermediary.

- to develop analytical skills and general understanding of the disciplines in which information is to be provided.
- to provide information solutions rather than volumes of literature that contain solutions.

Libraries, once basically repositories of vast quantities of information, are today becoming producers of information. In the digitization process major issues are : (1) text selection, (2) data conversion, (3) data presentation, (4) access, (5) archiving, and (6) education and training. The last twenty-five years have seen major changes in the way information is stored, and those changes have had a significant impact on the nature of the library and its services. Baker summarizes developments in Information technology and suggests that libraries will evolve in one of the four ways: (1) the polymedia library, (2) the electronic library, (3) the digital library, or (4) the virtual library.

Selection of electronic resources for libraries is similar in many ways to selection of print resources, but involves issues that are far more complex. Johnson recommends the development of an electronic resources policy statement including selection criteria and guidelines for evaluating and choosing electronic resources. The context of the local library is very important, and the development of local procedures for dealing with selected electronic resources is essential. The electronic environment for storing and using information is at hand, and is causing publishers, librarians, and users of information to take a serious look at past and present distribution practices. The electronic environment for storing and using information is at hand, and is causing publishers, librarians, and users of information to take a serious look at past and present distribution practices.

The behaviour of academic library users has drastically changed in recent years. Internet search engines have become the preferred tool over the library online public access catalog (OPAC) for finding information. Libraries are losing ground to online search engines. In this paper, two aspects of OPAC use are studied: (1) the current OPAC interface and searching capabilities, and (2) the OPAC bibliographic display. The purpose of the study is to find answers to the following questions: Why is the current OPAC ineffective? What can libraries and librarians do to deliver an OPAC that is as good as search engines to better serve our users? Revitalizing the library OPAC is one of the pressing issues that have to be accomplished.

It is technology and rising user expectations that have contributed to the changes in user behaviour. As Coyle and Hillman pointed out: "Today's library users have a different set of information skills from those of just a few decades ago. They live in a highly interactive, networked world and routinely turn to Web search engines for their information needs. The traditional catalog retrieval mechanism is significantly different."

The increased access to electronic information systems not held locally and to other new technologies such as CD-ROM, laser technologies, interactive multimedia packages, OCR (Optical Character Recognition) and imaging systems, satellite communication and teleconferencing, laptop computers, packet telephone switches, and cellular telephones have also been making an impact in a few libraries along with LANs (Local Area Networks) and WANs (Wide Area Networks) for interconnecting local computing resources.

The impact has not been only on more technologically oriented methods of operations and services; new information and instructional technologies have placed tremendous pressures on outdated cabling and wiring. Expanded budgets are required for such things as asbestos abatement in ceiling and floor tiling as well as utility tunnels; installation of fiber optics and additional connective wiring and cabling within and among buildings; and equipment (hardware and software) for both staff and public access. Additional funding is needed for online network memberships and connections to local, state, regional, national and international networks. These network relationships require new and expanded licensing agreements with updated copyright procedures and related issues. New formats and access tools require revamped policies and procedures, rules and regulations. Expanded training (of staff and users) and continuing education require icreased travel budgets for participation in new professionals.

10

Information Seeking Behaviour

People take action to satisfy their need when a need is felt for something. They resort different strategies or modes of action to satisfy their needs. The same applies to information needs. An individual realizes that he needs information and he knows pretty well that information will not come on its own. Therefore he has to go or about seeking the information.

Introduction

Information is the life blood of the society. Information is the foundation for generating knowledge. Each citizen of the world has right to have information. It is information that brings change in society. Therefore the terms information, knowledge are used synonymously. In other words information is knowledge and knowledge is information Any social development needs information.

We are living in an age of information; every government is now mainly concerned with the development of knowledge based institutions for purpose of creating, transmitting and utilizing the information for the overall development of the nation. Variety of information is generated by the institutions and they are needed to be moved from point of generation to the point of use. Information has no value until it is used.

Information - Definitions

The word information is used to identify many concepts. However, it is extremely difficult to define it precisely. But an understanding of how different individuals have tried to define and quantify information is valuable. Many definitions have been attempted but not even a single agreeable definition comprehending all its aspects have been arrived so far. According to Hayes." It is agreed that 'information' is a slippery concept amorphous, loaded with connotations and implications and that it has had a variety of meanings and we must have a suitable definition even if it is at the most elementary level." The simple meaning of information in a restricted sense is a sensible statement, opinion, fact, concept or idea, or an association of statements opinions or ideas. It is more important to define and analyze the term "information" for understanding the nature and concept of the term. Many definitions have been attempted in this regard.

Webster's New International Dictionary, 3rd edition, defines information as "the communication or reception of knowledge or intelligence". L. Brillorium viewed that "information is raw material and consists of mere collection of data."

Hoshvosky and Marsey view information as data used to solve problems. They consider information as a process which occurs within human mind when a problem and data for its solution are brought into productive union. The information is data of value in decision-making. Some authors treat information as message.

J.H. Shera also has the similar view when he says that information should also bring a response in the recipient. He says further, "In generic sense it is that which is transmitted by act or processes of communication. It may be a message a signal, or stimulus. It assumes a response in the receiving organism and therefore possesses response potential" In the context of users studies research, the term information is used to denote a physical entity or phenomenon (as in the case of questions relating to number of journals subscribed to etc.); the channel of communication through which messages are transferred (as when we speak of the incidence of oral versus written information), or the factual data, empirically determined and presented in a document or transmitted orally.

Davis, G.B. (1974) defined information as "data that has been processed into a form that is meaningful to the recipient and is of real perceived value in current or projective decision." Stevens (1986) defined information as the "factual data ideas and other knowledge emanating from any segment of society that identified as being of value, some fashion, transmitted to others, and used in some meaningful fashion."

Kent (1979) states that "Information is the feed-stock of knowledge. In an ideal world of unimpeded flow of information amongst individuals of equal capacity to process the information into knowledge, there would be no advantage to be gained by any individual or group as compared with another by possession of information."

As per Encyclopedia of Library and Information Science "a sophisticated definition emphasizes information as both a commodity and a process. Thus information as commodity has to be acted upon by an energy system in order to make it useful and allow it to be put into action. (i.e., transferred)."

Knowledge and information are often used interchangeably but some authors are able to make difference between these two terms. Farradane makes difference between these two terms, information is physical surrogate of knowledge (i.e. language) used for communication While knowledge is memorable records of process in the brain, something available in the mind is at present quite unexplained.

Nature of Information

Wilson Alex stated that "The nature and amount of information that effects the behaviour of a person (i. e. recipient) in taking the decision however varies from person to person, from time to time and from place to place. As such information is a resource of immense economic and social value. It is vital to the proper functioning of a democratic society, a crucial tool in a productive economy and also for an effective government, a central part of the growth and well beings of individuals".

The increasing need and dependence on information and the increase in technological sophistication and the complexities of modern social life have increased its nature and value. The nature and value of information is directly related to its communication. According to Viswanathan, "Information communicated could be broadly grouped into three categories:

1. Development; 2. Pedagogic; 3. Achievement; when one uses a document for general cultural advancement for enlargement of his vision; and for intellectual enjoyment, the information obtained is developmental; when a student studies a prescribed text-book or refers to an index, with a view to supplement the class instruction the information communicated is pedagogic; if a scientist working in a laboratory refers to abstract and indexes relating to the field of investigation or experiment, the information received is achievement in quality.

Principles and Qualities of Information

The ideas underlined in the five laws of library science enunciated by S.R. Ranganathan are the basic concepts of librarianship. Based on the five laws of library science, Bhattacharya has conceived five principles of information viz. "1. Information is for use. 2. Every information user his/her information. 3. Every piece of information its user. 4. Save the time of the information user. 5. The universe of information is ever growing."

As information is an important valuable resource, it ought to have certain ideal qualities also. According to Roja's "Some of the qualities of information are:

1. Accessibility. 2. Comprehensiveness. 3. Precision. 4. Compatibility. 5. Timelessness. 6. Clarity. 7. Flexibility. 8. Verifiability. 9. Free of bias and 10. Quantifiable."

William, F. William has recognized 6 parameters of information. They are :

"*Quality of information:* Which can be measured by the number of documents, pages, words, characteristics bits, drawings, etc.?

Content: Meaning of information.

Structure: The organization of information.

Language: Symbol, alphabets, codes.

Quality: Which characterizes the completeness, accuracy, relevance, and timeliness of information; and

Life: The total span of time in which value can be derived from the information."

In view of the different definitions, Mc Grarry summarizes varied attributes to see the nature of "information" "1. Information can be regarded as a near synonym of fact. 2. It had a transforming or reinforcing effect on what is known, or believed to be known, by a human being. 3. Information is used as an aid in decision-making. 4. Information is the freedom of choice one has in selecting a message. 5. Information is a necessary piece of something when we are faced with a choice. The amount required depends upon the complexity of decision to be made. 6. Information is the raw material from which knowledge is derived. 7. Information is exchanged with outer world; not merely received. 8. Information can be defined in terms of its effect on the recipient." It is clear that information is complex in contents, having more than one attribute to arrive at agreed definition, encompassing all its attributes seems difficult. In order to overcome such difficulty, the distinction is made between data, information and knowledge. Information falls between data and knowledge. Information can be perceived as something between data and knowledge which is communicated or received concerning a particular fact or circumstance in order to reduce the user's uncertainty by meeting their needs. The concept of information is fundamentally associated with human communication of recorded potential information, processed by generation as well as recipient.

Need and Purpose of Information

Information involves reduction of uncertainty, i.e., what the decision-maker expects from the information system. However, the degree of uncertainty of the decision-maker will vary, and so the amount of information needed or taken from the system will vary. Information is thus a relative quality, and can be quantified in terms of its effects on the state of decision-maker at a particular moment of time.

The amount of information needed to change the state of the decision-maker or alter his level of understanding a particular minimum amount of data is called an 'inform'. This minimum quantity of information will vary depending on the person, time and the place.

Needs Defined

The Encyclopedia of Psychology has given a comprehensive and clear explanation of the term 'need'. "Need is one of the several English words (the others being drive, motive, want, urge, desire and so on), each in some respects unsuitable used by psychologists today to designate an internally or externally aroused, brain located force (often coupled with an accelerating emotion), subjectively experienced as an impulsion or felt necessity (a mild or intense urge) to act (immediately or later) so as to produce a certain specifiable terminal effect which is ordinarily expected to be beneficial to the actor, and/or positively hedonic (less painful, more pleasurable) relative to the arousing situation.

Human needs are of two types: Physical and Psychological

Physical needs are requirements for mental health (e.g. self-esteem, pleasure)

According to Maslow the different types of human needs are :

Self actualizing needs: Formal education, leisure activities, ethics, values, etc.

Esteem needs: Multicultural awareness, emotional awareness, social system knowledge (legal, economic etc.), sex education, ethics, values etc.

Love and belonging needs: Multicultural awareness, emotional awareness, leisure activities, interpersonal skills, ethics and values, sex education etc.

Safety needs: Crime avoidance, traffic rules, emergency procedures, basic literacy, sex education etc.

Physiological needs: Person hygiene, nutrition, general health issues, aids prevention, drug, tobacco and alcohol abuse child abuse, sex education

Want: What a person would like to have

Demand: What a person asks for

Requirement: This can cover need, want and demand

The Difference Between 'Need' and 'Want'

One basic difference between need and want is that—person may not need what he wants Green finds that the element that most clearly distinguishes a need from a want or a demand is that there is no necessary self-awareness of a need. People frequently need things without being aware of the need.

Line is of the opinion that people do not feel a want for all they need to help them in their study or for that matter their gardening and they sometimes want what they do not need. We all like foods that are not good for us; a drug user needs to be helped off drugs but rarely wants. Likewise people do not always demand what they want, often because they do not expect to get it.

Information Needs

The next step is to understand the meaning of the term 'information need' though people differ in their information requirements, it is undeniable fact that no one can survive with-out some sort of information need. Farmers, businessmen, doctors, engineers, librarians, students, researchers, teachers—all are in need of information for their day to day survival. They ought to have information for their survival and struggle in their existence. They cannot live successfully without information. Information is essential for any individuals' health and well being.

Some attempts have been made at defining the term.

Line (1998) is on the opinion that all people will seek and use information in different ways. Most part of the daily life is spent in information gathering and shifting of one kind or another – mere looking at the people involves an information process, since things are noticed about them and a rapid assessment is done. Most of this information process is carried out automatically. There is no such thing homogenous body of information users.

Menzel suggested that "Information needs are not synonymous with either demands or conscious - wants of information users. It is not the information that users are aware of wanting that counts, not even the information that would be good for the best but rather the information that would be good for science - the progress of scientific research."

Brittain stated that the word 'information needs' is very difficult to define. In some cases needs are more difficult. In some cases needs are synonymous with demands: for example, when the user knows of all the that is relevant to his work and makes a demand for information sources. At the other extreme the user who makes very few demands has but many needs. Brittain identified 3 types of needs :

"1. An articulated need. 2. A felt but unarticulated need for any reason. 3. An unfelt need. In regard to the latter need users are unaware that they have a need until it is pointed out at which time they may readily agree to the need or they may not realize this until the need has actually been met."

Gronin divided user needs into 3 categories :

"1. Expressed needs.

2. Unexpressed needs.

3. dormant needs."

According to Line, "Information that the faculty member ought to have for his work, his research, his edification etc."

Ching-Chin Chen and Peter Hernon stress that information need is more than a question asked of an information provider. It occurs whenever people find themselves in situations that require some form of knowledge for resolution.

The librarian's Thesaurus defines information need as "that need which library services or materials are intended to satisfy".

Methods of Determining Information Needs

According to Soper "Community analysis is one method used by librarians to identify characteristics of a target population and to decide what library services and information would be more appropriate for them. The techniques that are used in community analysis include observing environmental characteristics, studying demographics, observing patterns of library use interviewing key formats."

Greer and Haire also support community analysis as the basis for determining a library's role. Their method involves data collection and analysis from our perspectives: demographics, community organizations, service-and-product-providing agencies and life styles.

Grover has presented a conceptual model for diagnosing information needs in the context of a school library media programme. He proposes a two-stage process: systematic analysis of both the school and the community followed by one-on-one interaction with a user at the point when he or she has decided to seek information, i. e., the reference interview. He asserts that the reference interview can become a vehicle for diagnosing information need by applying knowledge of information psychology - how individuals seek, acquire, organize, process, utilize and store information.

Dervin's sense-making methodology is one of the most widely adopted techniques for conducting needs assessments. The researcher tries to find out, with the help of timeline interviews, about the effort put in by an individual to acquire information in order to bridge a gap in a particular critical incident.

Factors Affecting Information Needs

By far the most important factor the information needs of an individual is the type of work in which he is involved - as found by Lin and Garvey. Another factor (relating to type of work), is – whether the work is basic or applied.

The discipline within which an individual is working also affects his information needs, for example, the information needs of researchers in the pure sciences is probably more urgent than that of researchers in the social sciences, because science is ever growing. The scientist will need to constantly update his knowledge, i.e. he has to catch-up with the latest developments.

Other factors include-social, political, economic and legal.

Concepts of Information Seeking Behaviour

ISB is an integral part of the human beings personality and they all perform it differently. A group of people with the same level of education may be working on the same subject at the same time. But they will use the information in different ways. Some information may obviously be relevant to all of them. Some information to only one or two. Some persons of the group will scan and absorb a vast amount of information. Others will read a little. Some persons will be content with abstracts of many articles. Some will prefer oral channels. Somebody prefers to see information in print so that they can pore over it. Someone always asks other people. Some persons prefer to avoid people whenever they can. Some persons like browsing and some find it as mere waste of time. Some persons enjoy computer searching. When people search for information on internet they do it differently.

Information Seeking Behaviour Definitions and Meaning

Different authors have defined the Information seeking concept in different ways. Taylor (1991) defined information seeking behaviour as the product of the certain elements of the information use environment. They are:

- The assumption formally learned or not made by a defined set of people.
- The kinds of structure of problems thought to be important and typical by the people.
- The constraints and opportunities of typical environments within which any group or sub-group of the set of people operates and works.

- The conscious and unconscious assumptions made as to what constitutes a solution or a resolution of problems and what makes information useful and valuable in their contexts.

Based on the definitions Taylor inferred that Information seeking behaviour of different group of people are also different.

Wilson (1999) defined Information seeking behaviour is as those activities a person may engage in identifying his or her own needs for information, searching for such information in any way and using or transferring information.

From the above definitions it is observed that information is a stimulus that reduces uncertainty. Where as need is defined as recognition of the existence of this uncertainty in the personal or work related life of an individual.

Atkins (1973) defined information need as a function of extrinsic uncertainty produced by a perceived discrepancy between the individual's current level of uncertainty about important environmental objects and certain state he seeks to achieve. In other words, Information seeking begins when some one perceives that the current state of possessed knowledge is less than that he needed to deal with some problem or issue. The process ends when the perception no longer exists.

From the above definitions the following inferences are drawn :

- Information seeking behavior is mainly concerned with who needs what kind of information.
- It is an activity of an individual in pursuit of information.
- Information seeking behaviour is related to personal characteristics of the users.

Information Seeking Behaviour Models

Many models on information seeking behaviour have been framed to explain the information seeking behaviour and

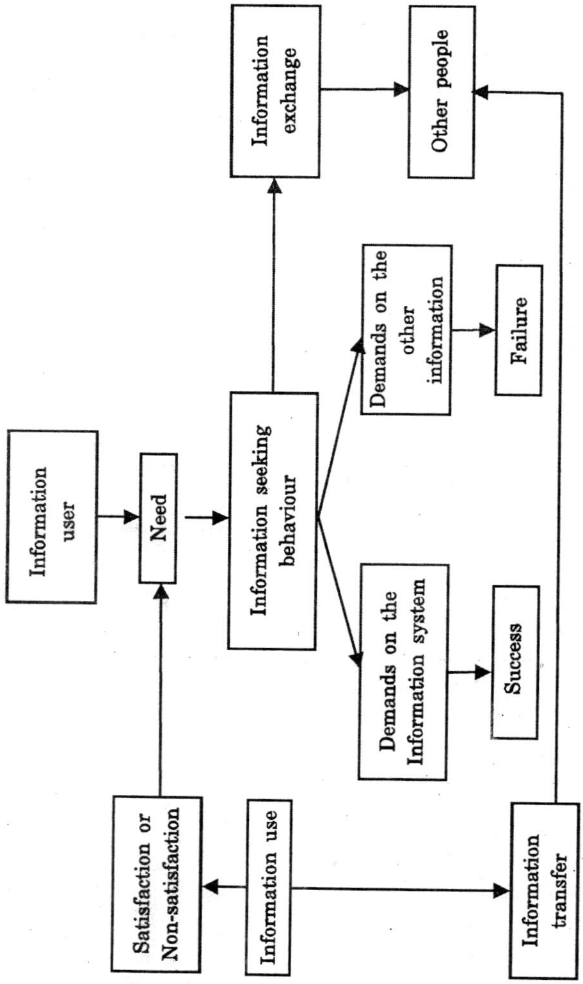

Fig. 10.1 : Wilson's Model of Information seeking behaviour (1981).

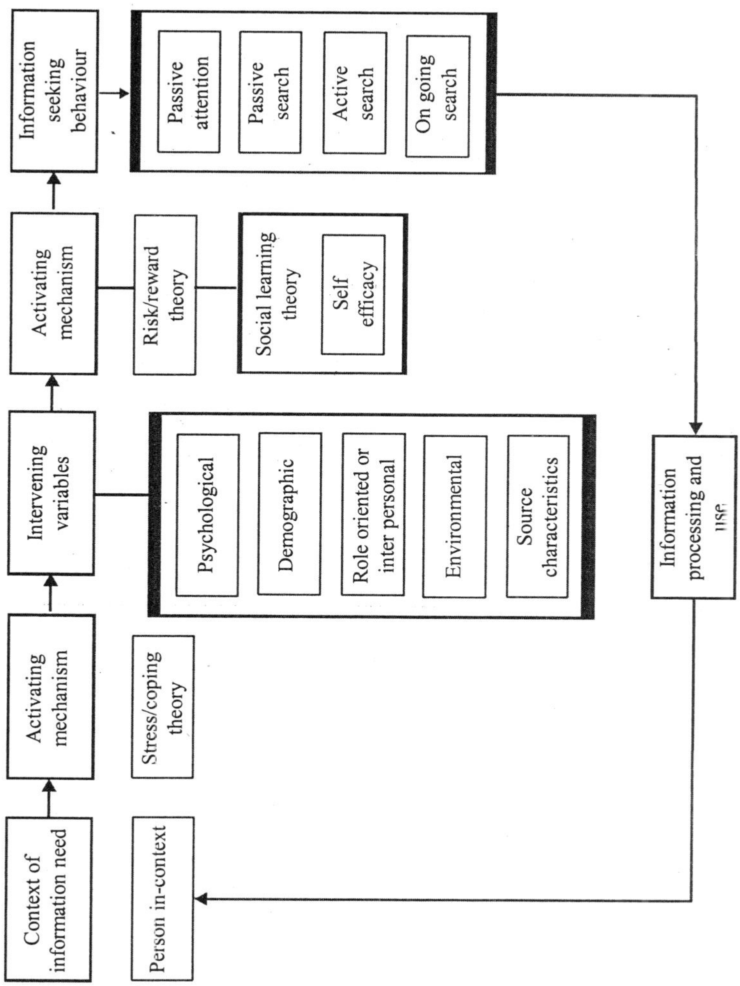

Fig. 10.2 : Wilson's 1996 model of Information behaviour

process. A model is framework for thinking on a problem and it may evolve into a statement of the relationships among theoretical propositions. Simply in other words models are statements, diagrams that describe the information seeking function, the reasons for that function or the relationship among states in information seeking behaviour. Some of the models that have been developed are presented in this study. Wilson (1981) was the first researcher to present the concept of information seeking behaviour. His model of Information seeking behaviour delineates that information seeking commences with need and the ISB in the model ends with success or failure to get the desired information.

Wilson's model suggests that due to the need perceived by an information user information seeking behaviour arises. To satisfy that need he makes demands on the formal or informal information sources or services, resulting in success or failure to find relevant information. If succeeds, he makes use of the information found and may fully or partially satisfies the perceived need. If he fails to satisfy the need, he will have to search again. This model also shows that part of the information seeking behaviour may involve other people through information exchange and the information perceived as useful may be passed to other people as well as being used by himself.

Girija Kumar (1990) presentation of the information seeking process is as follows :

(i) Identifying objectives.

(ii) Defining need.

(iii) Assessing information systems.

(iv) Establishing sources of information.

(v) Information acquisition.

(vi) Use of Information.

(vii) Satisfaction/Dissatisfaction.

Wilson (1996) revised the earlier model after drawing upon research from a variety of fields other than information science, including decision-making, psychology, innovation, health communication and consumer research. Additions in Figure 10.3.

The terms in the new model are as follows: *"intervening variables"* represent the Barriers' whose impact may be supportive of information use as well as preventive. Information seeking behaviour is shown to consist of more types than previously, information processing and use is shown to be necessary part of the feed back loop if information needs are to be satisfied.

The *stress/coping* theory tries to explain why some needs do not invoke information seeking behaviour. The risk/reward theory tries to explain which sources of information may used more than others by a given individual and the social learning theory embodies the concept of self-efficacy, i.e., the conviction that one can successfully execute the behaviour required to produce the [desired] outcome. Wilson (1997) suggested a general information behaviour model that needs to include the minimum three elements.

- An information need and its drives, i.e. the factors that give raise to an individual's perception of need.
- The factors that affect the individuals response to the perception of need.
- The process of actions involved in that response.

Ellis (1989) and Ellis, Cox and Hall (1993) use the term features 'instead of stages' in information seeking. They are:

Starting : The means employed by the user to begin information seeking, for example, asking a knowledge colleague.

Chaining : Following footnotes and citations in known material or forward chaining from known items through citation indexes.

Browsing : Semi-directed or semi-structured searching.

Differentiating : Using known differences in information sources as a way of filtering the amount of information obtained.

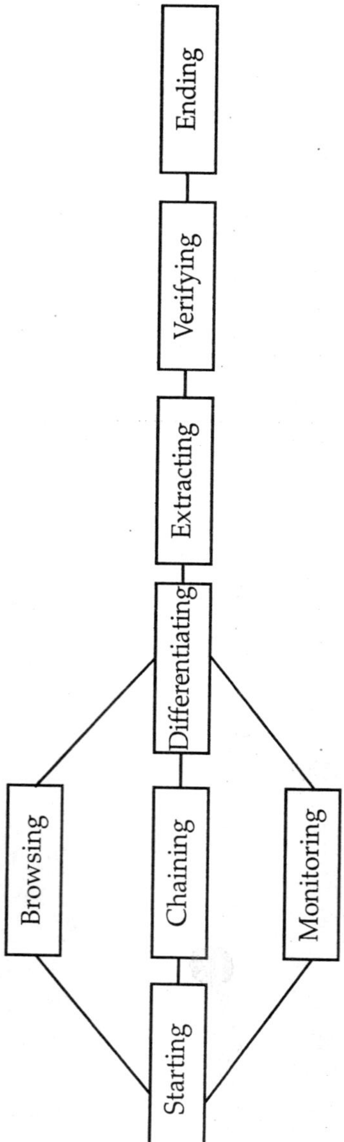

Fig.10.3 : Ellis's Behavioural Framework.

Monitoring : Keeping up-to-date or current awareness searching.

Extracting : Selectively identifying relevant material in information source.

Verifying : Checking the accuracy of the information.

Ending : *i.e.* the tying up of loose ends through a final search.

Leckie (1996) developed a model of information seeking by professionals. It discusses about several components of information seeking by General Practitioners: work roles, associated tasks of general practitioners, characteristics of their information needs, the factors affecting information seeking-sources, awareness and conduct. Figure 10.4 shows the Information seeking behavior of Leckie.

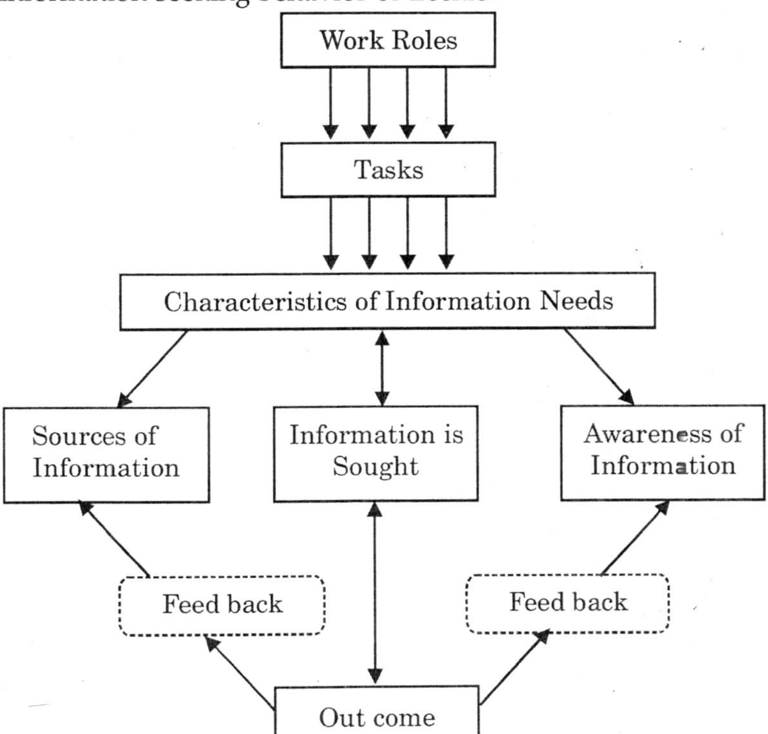

Fig. 10.4 : Information seeking model by Leckie, G.J.

Auguilar (1967) developed Information seeking model based on the four modes of scanning on the web like undirected viewing, conditioned viewing, informal searching and formal search.

Scanning Modes	*Information Needs*	*Information Seeking*	*Information use*
Undirected viewing	General areas of interest specific need to be revealed	* Scan broadly a diversity of sources, taking advantage of what is easily accessible *"Sweeping"	Serendipitous discovery
Conditioned viewing	Able to recognize topics of interest	Browse in pre-selected sources on prescribed topics of interest *"Discriminating"	Increase knowledge about topics of interest *"Learning"
Informal search	Able to formulate simple questions	Search is focused on areas of topic, but a good enough search is Satisfactory	Increase knowledge on area, within narrow boundaries "Selecting"
Formal search	Able to Specify Targets in details	Systematic gathering of Information about an entity following some method or procedure "Optimizing"	Formal use of information for decision-policy making "Retrieving"

Fig. 10. 5 : Auguliar Francis J. ISB model on the web.

Choo (1999) presented their findings from a study of how knowledge workers use the web to seek external information. They developed a behavioural model of information seeking on the web based on the modes of browsing and searching, differentiated by information needs and information seeking activities (fig.10.6). They combined the Auguliar's four modes

	Starting	*Chaining*	*Browsing*	*Differentiating*	*Monitoring*	*Extracting*
Undirected Viewing	Identifying selecting starting pages, sites	Following links on initial pages				
Conditioned Viewing			Browsing entry pages, headings, site maps	Bookmaking, printing, copying Going directly to known site	Revisiting 'favourite' or book marked sites for new information	
Informal Search				Bookmaking, printing, copying Going directly to known site	Revisiting 'favourite' or bookmarked site for new information	Using (local) search engines to extract information
Formal Search					Revisiting 'favourite' or bookmarked sites for new information	Using search engines to extract information

Fig. 10.6 : Behavioural Modes and Moves of Information Seeking on the Web of Choo.

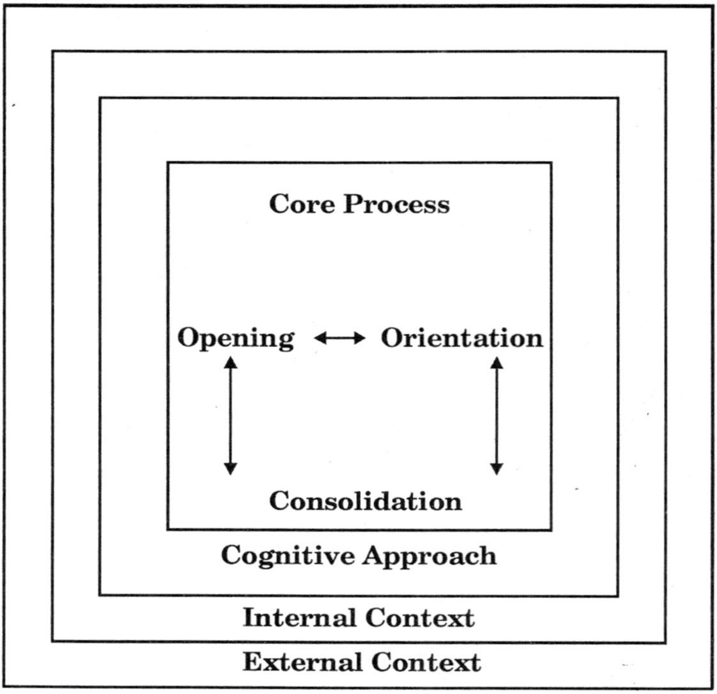

Fig.10.7 : Inter disciplinary Information seeking model of Forster.

of scanning and Elli's Information seeking behaviour model to extend a new behavioural model of information seeking on the web.

Forster (2005) developed a new model of Inter-disciplinary information seeking by grouping the emergent concepts into three core categories: Opening, Orientation and Consolidation around which details relating to their definition function and context continued to be developed through analysis.

Choo (1999) further developed Information seeking process model with three major steps, namely: 1.Information needs 2. Information seeking 3. Information use.

Loeber (2003) extended the Information seeking process model of choo. It still consists of three major steps, particularly suits to navigate in the WWW.

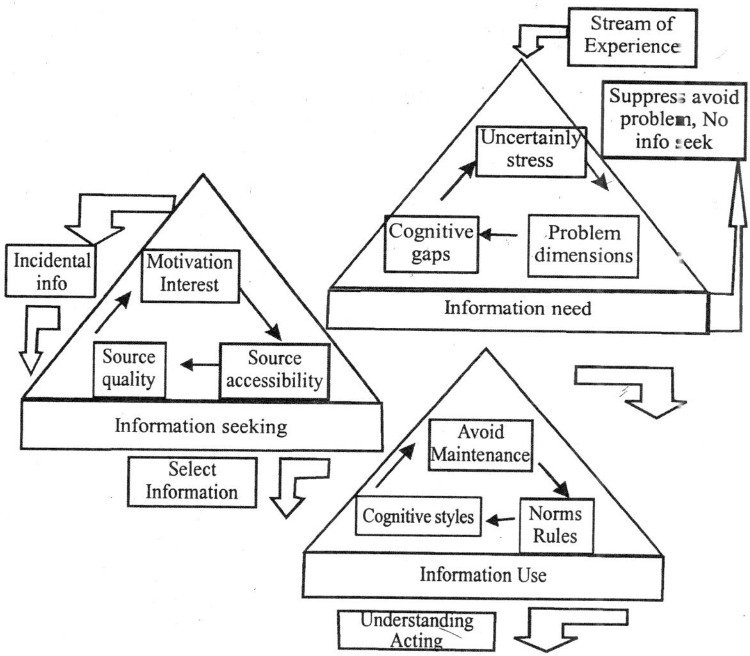

Fig.10. 8 : Choo (1999) Information Seeking Process model

INFORMATION SEEKING BEHAVIOUR

Swarnalatha Devi and Lahiri (1997) made a survey of information seeking behaviour of 40 Agricultural Scientists working in ICAR, Manipal, College of Agriculture and Manipur University. The study revealed that the Agricultural Scientists seek information for research, experiments and appear writing, most of the scientists prefer 'paper publication' as the better medium for dissemination of their results. A sizeable section however favours other media like 'radio talk' or 'demonstration to the formers' and a major section of the scientists, agricultural information available in the state is minimum.

Tripathi and Prasad (1998) conducted a survey on reports results of a questionnaire survey, undertaken by Banaras Hindu University, to determine the similarities and differences

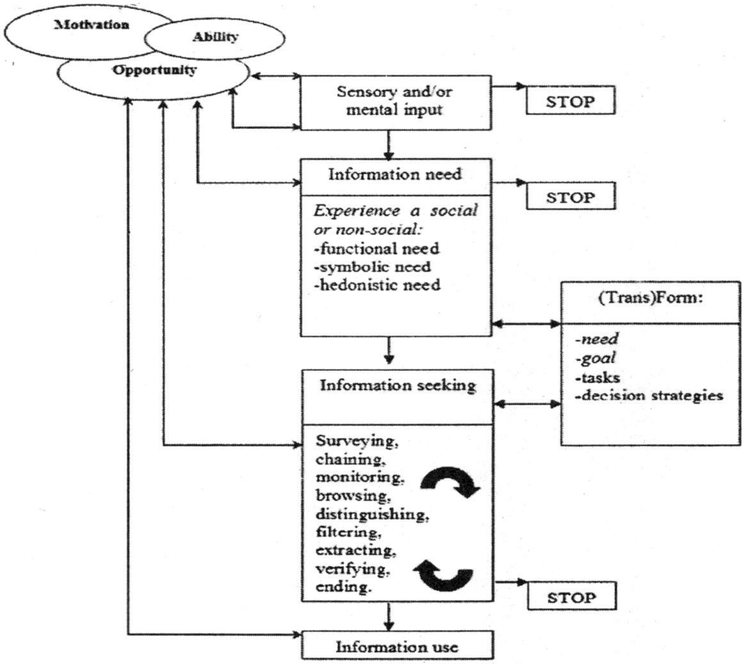

Fig. 10.9 : Loeber's Information seeking process model.

between the information seeking behaviour of physical scientists and social scientists. The study investigated the use of formal and informal channels of information, tools and techniques used for current awareness publication output, use of materials available in languages other than English, types of information used and frequency of visits to the library. Concludes that there are significant differences between the two groups and summarizes their main characteristics.

Tripathi and Prasad, (2001) conducted a survey which deals with the information seekng behaviour of scientists in physical and social sciences. Highlights various sources and methods followed by the scientists to locate require information. Discusses various types of information and bibliographical sources used by the scientists in the study.

Bibliography

1. Abell, A. and Oxbrow, N. (2001) : Competing with knowledge: the information professional in the knowledge management age. London: Library Association publishing.
2. Abhijit Lahri and Sunder Singh B. G. : Bibliographic Database NISSAT News letter, 8(2) 1989, pp. 3-76.
3. Ananad, C.M. and Sen B. K. : Man Power development for Computer Application Library and Information Activities IASLIC Bulletin, 36(4), 1991, pp. 157-169.
4. Aruna A : On-Line Public Access Catalogue. DESIDOC Bulletin of Information Technology, 18 (5), 1998.
5. Adams. Roy J : Information Technology and Libraries. London, Croom Helm, 1986, pp. 1-57.
6. Cater Roser: The Information Technology Handbook, London, Heinemann Professional, 1987.
7. Croud, J., et. al, (2002) : From lackey to leader: the evolution of the librarian in the age of the Internet, available at: www.Librart.uq.edu.au/papers/from_lackey_to_leader.pdf
8. Haravu, L. J. : Library Automation: Design principles and practice. Allied Publishers, New Delhi, 2004.
9. Gopinath, M. A. : Application of Information Technology. New Delhi, IGNOU, 1995 (Course Material).
10. Humes, Understanding Information Literacy.
11. Kaul, H. K. : Library Network : An Indian Experience USA, Storicus Inc. 1993.
12. Lancaster, F.W. : Electronic Publishing, Library Trends: CLIRE Bingby Illinois, 1998, pp. 315–325.

13. Lowry, Charles, B. : Resource Sharing College Research Libraries North America Inc., BLACKWELL, 1991.

14. Maria, G.M. (2007) : Librarians in the age of the internets: their attitudes and roles: A Literature review. New Library World 108, 3/4.123-140.

15. Madan Somnath: Computer and Library Services, DELHI; INSDOC 1991.

16. Murthy, S. S. : Use of I.T. in Library and Information Science Education. DESIDOC Bulletin of Information Technology 16(3). 1997, p. 3.

17. Rajan, T. and Satynarayana: Application of Information technologies in India problems and Perspectives. Annals of Library Science and Documentation 30 (3-4) 1983. pp. 134-150.

18. Rajasekhar, T. B. : Computer Software for Library and Information Work Problems and Prospects for India. IASLIC Bulletin, 31 (4), 1986, pp. 135-142.

19. Rajasekhar, T. S. : Computer Assisted Library and Information Management. Annals of Library Science and Documentation. 30(314) 1983, pp. 105-133.

20. Ramesh Babu, B., and Gopalkrishnan, S. (2008) : Changing Dimensions of Libraries as Knowledge Centres: Role of Librarians. IN B. Ramesh Babu et al. (Eds). Library Resources and Services in the Digital Era. Kancheepuram: SRM University.

21. Ramesh Babu, B. and Ramesha (2007) : Soft Skills for Library and Information Science (LIS) professional's professionals in the knowledge society. IN M.M. Koganurmath et al. (Eds), Library and Information Science professor in the knowledge society (Festschrift Volume) (pp. 331-339), New Delhi, Allied.

22. Ramakrishna Reddy D. Y. K. : Computerized Document Circulation. IASLIC Bulletin 42 (2), 1997.

23. Rama Devi, B: Information technology and Information Services–A scenario. DESIDOC Bulletin, 2(3), 1991, pp. 3-8.

24. Rashid Abdul: Implementing and Managing Information Technology Guidelines for Libraries. Library Science with a Slant to Documentation and Information Studies 35(2), pp. 117-123.

25. Sailendra Kumar and Neosi, B. M. : Perspective and Role of Information Development in 7th Five Year Plan of CSIR. IASLIC Bulletin 30(3), 1987, pp. 117-213.

26. Satynanarayana, V.V.V. (et al): Application of Information Technology, Hyderabad, MIS Art Waves, 1998 (Dr. Ambedkar Open University).

27. Sen B. K. Information Technology Curriculum for Library and Information Science Course at INSDOC, New Delhi. Library Science with Slant to Documentation 27(2) 199, pp. 60-80.

28. Shapiro, Jeremy J. ad Hughes, K. Shelley : Information Literacy as a Liberal Art, enlightment proposals for a new curriculum.

29. Sunil Kumar, Satpaathy and et al : Modernization of Libraries: A Challenge in Digital Era; Mahamaya Publishers, New Delhi, 2008.

30. Willis, Jerry and Merl Miller: Computers for Everybody, BPB Publications, Delhi, 1987.

WEB SITES REFERENCES

http://net.educause.edu/apps/er/review/reviewArticles/31231.html

http://www.newhorizons.org/strategies/technology/dede1.htm#implications

http://en.wikipedia.org/wiki/List_of_search_engines

http://www.informationliteracy.ie/

http://www.swan.ac.uk/lis/

http://www.library.uq.edu.au/internet/subject_gateways1.html

http://igmlnet.uohyd.ernet.in:8000/subject.htm

http://publications.drdo.gov.in/gsdl/collect/dbit/index/assoc/HASH85adir/dbit202003.pdf

http://www.hw.ac.uk/libwww/irn/pinakes/pinakes.html

http://en.wikipedia.org/wiki/Academic_journal#CITEREFHendler200# CITEREFHendler2007

http://crl.du.ac.in/Details%20of%20E-Resources%20Subscribed%20by%20DULS.htm

www.google.co.in

http://en.wikipedia.org/wiki/Main_Page

http://information-literacy. blogspot.com/

http://infolitweb.blogspot.com/

http://acrlog.org/2007/01/31/journal-of-information-literacy/

Videos on Information Literacy @ http://www.youtube.com

Index

J

T